REAL ESTATE
INVESTING ROCK STARS

JIM HUNTZICKER

Copyright Notice

Copyright © 2015 by J.P. Huntz, Inc.

All rights reserved.

No part of this publication may be reproduced or transmitted in any form or by any means—mechanical or electronic, including photocopying and recording— or by any information storage and retrieval system without permission in writing from the publisher. Requests for permission or further information should be addressed to J.P. Huntz, Inc.

Jim Huntzicker (Illinois Licensed Realtor)

J.P. Huntz, Inc.

925 N Plum Grove Rd Unit G

Schaumburg, IL 60173

www.RealEstateInvestorAcademy.com

Legal Notice

While all attempts have been made to verify information provided in this publication, neither the author nor the publisher assumes any responsibility for errors, omissions, or contrary interpretation of the subject matter.

This publication is not intended for use as a source of legal or accounting advice. The publisher stresses that the information contained herein may be subject to varying state and/or local laws or regulations. All users are advised to retain competent counsel to determine state and/or local laws or regulations that may apply to the user's particular business.

The purchaser or reader of this publication assumes responsibility for the use of the materials. Adherence to all applicable federal, state, and local laws and regulations governing professional licensing, business practices, advertising, and all other aspects of doing business in the United States or any other jurisdiction is the sole responsibility of the purchaser or reader. The author and publisher assume no responsibility or liability whatsoever on behalf of any purchaser or reader of the materials.

Any perceived slights of specific people or organizations are unintentional.

CONTENTS

Earnings and Income Disclaimer 7
Real Estate Investing Rock Stars 10
Than Merrill 15
Doug Clark 27
Chief Denney 41
Kent Clothier 58
Ron LeGrand 73
Zack Childress 89
Mark Evans, DM 100
Larry Goins 115
Mike Hambright 120
Matt Andrews 134
Alan Cowgill 149
Andrew Cordle 161
Jeff Watson 189
John Cochran 209
Gregg Cohen 219

Justin Colby	226
Tim Mai	232
Mitch Stephen	245
Chris Urso	257
Mike Wolf	264
Tucker Merrihew	274
Erik Stark	288
Ian Flannigan	298
Joe McCall	305
Matt Theriault	315
Danny Johnson	321
Wendy Patton	330
Joe Fairless	337
Garrett Gunderson	342
Jim Huntzicker	352

Earnings and Income Disclaimer

Any income or earnings statements are estimates of income potential only, and there is no assurance that your earnings will match the figures we present. Your reliance on the figures we present is at your own risk. Any income or earnings depicted are NOT to be interpreted as common, typical, expected, or normal for the average student. This particular result may be exceptional, and the variables that impact results are so numerous and sometimes uncontrollable, that RealEstateInvestorAcademy.com, MLS Domination and Jim Huntzicker makes no guarantees as to your income or earnings of any kind, at any time.

Where specific income figures are used, and attributed to an individual or business, those persons or businesses have earned that amount. But, there is no assurance that your earnings or income will match those figures, or that you will make any money at all. If you rely upon our examples or figures, you do so at your own risk, and you accept all risk associated with your reliance.

Any and all claims or representations as to income earnings made on our web sites or in our materials or information are not to be considered as average earnings. Testimonials are not representative.

There can be no assurances that any prior successes, or past results, as to income earnings, can be used as an indication of your future success or results.

Monetary and income results are based on many factors. We have no way of knowing how well you will do, as we do not know you, your background, your work ethic, or your business skills or practices. Therefore we do not guarantee or imply that you will win any incentives or prizes that may be offered, that you will make any income or earnings, that you will do well, or that you will make any money at all. If you rely upon our examples or figures, you do so at your own risk, and you accept all risk associated with your reliance.

Real property businesses and earnings derived therefrom, have unknown risks involved, and are not suitable for everyone. Making decisions based on any information presented in our programs, products, services or on our website, should be done only with the knowledge that you could experience significant losses, or make no money at all. Only risk capital should be used.

All products and services of our company are for educational and informational purposes only. Use caution and seek the advice of qualified professionals. Check with your accountant, lawyer or professional advisor, before acting on this or any information.

Users of our programs, products, services and website are advised to do their own due diligence when it comes to making business decisions and all information, programs, products and services that have been provided should be independently verified by your own qualified professionals. Our information, programs, products and services should be carefully considered and evaluated before reaching a business decision, or whether to rely on them. All disclosures and disclaimers made herein, on our web sites or in any materials provided to you apply equally to any offers, prizes or incentives that may be made by our company.

You agree that our company is not responsible for the success or failure of your business decisions relating to any information presented by our company, or our company programs, products and/or services.

REAL ESTATE INVESTING ROCK STARS

If you had the opportunity to ask 29 of the top real estate investors in the country 1 question, what would that question be?

I asked myself that very question. If I myself had the opportunity to ask 25 of the top real estate investors in the country one question (which I did), just 1, what would it be?

I found that there is only one question suitable for this situation and the basis for this entire book. Here is the question I asked them all:

> **"If you had to start your real estate investing business over from scratch today (without much money), knowing what you do now, what would you do first? What marketing strategy would you focus on?"**

Contained in this book are the transcripts from our conversation. This was just a couple of guys (and 1 gal) having a conversation. Some answers are quick and to the point and others went into more detail. All of the info is incredibly valuable and as a special bonus I snuck in an extra question. So after asking these rock stars the first question, if you could ask them 1 follow up question what would that be?

Well here is what I decided to ask them:

"If you could name just 1 productivity habit or tool you use on a daily basis to produce the results that you do, what would you say that is?"

Yes, you're welcome ☺ This was a question I actually asked selfishly. In the middle of the first interview I came up with it and threw it out and then I asked every one of these rock stars the same question. The answers are as good as the answers to the original question (some better in my opinion).

As real estate investors, we are all entrepreneurs. We all suffer from shiny object syndrome. Didn't you know a requirement to enter the entrepreneurial world is a severe case of ADD? I am of course kidding (sort of) but who better to ask what helps keep them on track then the top real estate minds in the country. There are answers from splashing cold water on your face as soon as you get up to some sweet goal setting strategies to awesome free apps and websites they use to keep their teams organized. Every answer from every one of these people is extremely valuable. I learned something in every single interview I did and I can't wait to do it again because it was such a great experience for me personally.

What an incredible experience to interview all of these people who are achieving at such high levels. We have guys in here who have done 3,000+ deals in their 32 year career and we have a guy whose company did 600 deals last year alone. There is an investor that did 1,300 seller-financed deals in the last 15 years and an investor who in the last 4 years raised over $18 million in private money and now controls over $50 million in apartment complexes all over the Midwest.

Or maybe you want to read about the guy that built such a successful wholesale business that he now runs his Ohio-based business while traveling the world with his wife. Maybe this guy will be more your speed. After flipping over 400 properties in Detroit in the last few years he decided one day that family and life style was more important so he up and moved to South Florida. You might want to read that one because he started a brand new real estate business when he got there so he answered my question from direct recent experience (FYI: the coolest part is he just turned 31).

I am sure HUD homes interest you, right? Well then you will have to read about the guy doing 3-4 HUD deals A weEK! And he just started doing it in 4 different states because his systems are so successful.

Also you will hear from people that are masters at rehabbing, wholesaling, lease options, sandwich lease options, wholesaling lease options, subject-tos, tax liens and MLS experts…people who teach and train on this stuff and others that just do it for a living (a VERY good living). I have got it all in the book. From Chicago to Ohio, New York, Florida, Texas, Alabama, Oregon, Indiana, California and everywhere in between. I have got people in here all over the country investing in real estate in every kind of market. Some even invest in markets they no longer live in; "virtual investing" if you will. Others went directly into markets in the country they knew were good for their type of investing.

And the best part is they all are going to tell you what they would do if they had to start over again today. The information contained in the book is priceless really. I don't care if you are a seasoned investor or just starting out. Everyone will take something away from reading this.

You will see some similarities between them but I think the thing that stood out the most to me are the ones that said to pick one thing and master it in your market (which everyone pretty much did on one level or another). We see so many new investors trying to be the jack of all trades but become the master of nothing. And as such, they fail. What I found during these interviews and off-line when we were speaking as well is that they ALL have one central investing focus. It might be wholesaling, rehabbing, lease options, seller financing, selling and managing turnkey cash flow, large apartment complexes, wholesaling lease options, buying HUD homes, tax liens…Whatever it is, what I realized about these guys that produce at a high level is they didn't re-invent the wheel. They went out and got really good at 1 form of real estate investing and made a crap load of money doing it. Then they keep doing that over and over and over…like printing their own money.

You will see many mention some version of wholesaling but they all have their own little twist as to what they do and how they do it. I did expect that many of the answers would relate back to wholesaling. That was not surprising to me. But the interesting part to me is all of the different responses on FREE marketing for sellers, cash buyers, and how to market for deals. I heard a ton of awesome strategies that are not "main stream" and I LOVED that.

I had a few of them ask me this: what if everyone says basically the same thing? They said that would be boring for the reader. I said, "No, I think that would be awesome for the reader. I mean if 25 of the top real estate investors in the country all said they would start their business over the exact same way, don't you think that might be EXTREMELY valuable information to have and just go and do that?"

To me, I would look at that as my next 3 days, 3 months, and 1 year business plan and goals if I was looking to start out again in this business.

That being said, there does happen to be a variety of different responses anyway… so not to worry.

I learned more in this interview series then I ever could have imagined about these rock stars but I also learned about myself too. It was powerful, inspiring, and motivating. I truly hope you get as much out of it as I did.

So here we go…

Than Merrill

Today we have with us somebody that will go down into the real estate rock n' roll hall of fame if he's not there already. We've got Than Merrill, who is star of A&E's 'Flip this House', Co-Founder of Fortune Builders and CT Homes. These guys started flipping houses in the East Coast if you're familiar with them, and now they're out in San Diego and just killing it.

Than is also the author of 'The Real Estate Wholesaling Bible'. On top of all this as if the guy hadn't accomplished enough, before all of this he actually played in the NFL. For me being from Chicago I love this, he was on the Bears for a season or two. We'll ask him about that in a second. He decided to not play in the NFL and the real estate investing business would be better suited for him. He now makes money keeping his body intact, sitting at his desk.

Than's Answer:

It's a very good question. There are a lot of different direct response campaigns that we run effectively and we've been running effectively for years. Everything from pre-foreclosure direct mail, to probate direct mail, to online lead generation. One of the cornerstones I have to say over the past decade of buying-selling homes has been the MLS. Most people know about the MLS, but they may not necessarily know ... I would say that the proper way to work and ...

I want to spend a little time maybe discussing the Multiple Listing Service, and really ... I want to first of all give people a scope of what happens in most areas. The majority of property, 80% of properties hit the MLS. It doesn't matter what market you're in, the majority of transactions are being sold on the MLS. Now there are a lot of bad deals on the MLS. There are a lot of retail deals. There are a lot of just transactions that happen between a seller who's not motivated and the retail buyer who is going to move into the property. That's probably the majority of transactions that unfold.

Just because of the sheer number of properties in every major market around the country that hit the MLS there's always going to opportunity. If you're an investor who's starting out and you don't have a lot of capital, which is the premise of the question. I think a key component of the question, if you ask Jim, is well what options do you have? If you don't have a lot of capital, you may only be able to do one or two direct mail campaigns. If you don't get a quick hit right away on a project, then you maybe up a creek without a paddle.

If I were to start all over again and without any capital whatsoever, I would consider looking at a working MLS. Here's really the difference I think in what we do that's a little different than maybe other investors out there. This will give people key insights whether you're a new investor or an experienced investor alike. What we do is we monitor the daily ... the MLS. We have two guys in our office every single day that's all they do. They are literally on the MLS all day long looking at the newly listed properties for that day and then calling the agents.

The first thing we do is we filter the MLS. We look at if 100 properties hit the MLS that day in our area, we'll probably call on 10% maybe 15% of the listings. We're looking for properties that generally fit into one of three categories. Either it's a newly listed short sale, a pre-foreclosure property that's clearly a short sale and has been identified and/or marked by the realtor as a short sale. Or it's an REO. Or it just has some visible signs of distress. Or that the realtor in the remarks or the confidential remarks that they make when they list the property, describes it as having distress in some way. Either the property itself or it could be a distress situation with the seller.

What we're doing is we're weeding out 85/90% of the properties that we know will sell at or around market value or close to it. We focus on the ones that we think will produce.

The other thing that we do, and this is kind of unique and it'll really depend on your market, is we also know that there are certain price points in certain areas of the city where there are unique opportunities. For example, we know in certain neighborhoods if we see a property listed below a certain price and it's a property that's below 1,500 square feet, that it may be an option of hey, we can create a second story on the house. Or we can add and addition and we can force the value of that property up significantly.

We have certain triggers that we look at as well based on values and based on square footage. A lot of investors don't even look at those types of projects or aren't even aware. They are just solely focused on is it distress, is it a short scale, something of that nature. The better you know your zoning, the better you know your values per square foot in an area, that will start to result in unique opportunities.

We'll buy homes that a lot of investors don't even look at that maybe let's say they're 1,300 square feet and we add an additional 1,000 square feet by putting a second story on the house. Yet the homes in that neighborhood are selling for significantly more than it costs us to create that second story or that addition. We're sometimes looking even at properties just from a development standpoint that may not hit the radar of other investors.

That's one opportunity, but the major opportunity we have with the MLS is just the speed at which we act and the relationships we build with realtors. A lot of investors who may have preconceived notions about the MLS will say, "There's not any deals on the MLS." There are absolutely deals on the MLS. Those deals are going to someone, and generally it's the investors who take the time to establish solid relationships with realtors in their area.

Every realtor in our area we consider them to be … They're like a small asset to our business. We take the time to build relationships with them. Get them to understand that we're an investment company and we're not necessarily going to be a great fit for every property that they may list. Maybe one out of five listings or one out of seven listings that they get was the perfect opportunity.

One of the things that we've really focused on over the past few years on the MLS in particular is short sales because a lot of … What's unique about short sales is there's a lot of investors who don't know how to work a short sale through an agent. They may be very skilled doing direct mail campaigns to sellers directly and working with the sellers directly and not having to worry about an agent being involved. A lot of agents naturally get pre-foreclosure listings.

We've become very adept at convincing the agents to work directly with us because think about this, if the property hits the market some short sales an agent will list the property for more than it's worth. It gets very few showings, very few, if any interests on the property. Now they have a seller who's on a very short timeline a lot of times that has to sell the property that needs to sell the property. They're not getting a lot of attention on that property because the agent listed it for more, plus their commission. They really out-priced what that property is worth.

A lot of times what we'll do is we'll reach out to that agent and say, "Hey listen, we're going to make an offer on the property. We're going to put this property under contract. It's still not going to be a solid deal until the bank approves the offer but we're going to go through the short sale process." The great thing about short sales that are listed by agents is a lot of retail buyers don't want to sit around and wait two/three/four months to figure out if a bank will accept their negotiated offer. Even if it's a higher offer than what we might present as investors, they just don't want to sit around and wait.

A lot of retail buyers it eliminates them from the equation on short sale properties. Whereas REOs that's a little different. You're going to get a little higher percentage of retail buyers may be willing to put an offer in on a retail or on an REO. We really found that to be a very profitable niche. That's probably the first type of property that I would focus on if I were starting all over again.

A lot of agents don't understand that if you don't an offer on the property, even if it's significantly lower than what the agent may think they could get if they waited around weeks or months. That gets the short sale process started. It gets the bank to take the file more seriously. The bank's gear's in motion to discuss that offer. Although we don't close on every single short sale property that we've put under contract on the MLS because sometimes the banks don't negotiate enough for the price that we're willing to pay.

At that point if the bank comes down but they don't come down enough, what we'll do is we'll just tell the agent, "Hey, here's the highest we're willing to go if we can't get the bank to agree to this price." At least now a lot of times they bank has given you a number that they're willing to accept and now you can turn around and we'll withdraw our offer. You can now go sell the property because you've gotten the bank to commit to a price.

A lot of agents really like working with us because they understand, although we may be taking a shot here and it may not come to fruition on every single transaction, it's going to allow me to know exactly what price I can sell that property at. I can then get that property sold whether it's to us as the buyer or to another buyer who's maybe willing to pay a little bit more for … more than us for the property.

That in a nutshell, I don't know if you have any questions about that Jim because I gave you a pretty longwinded answer-

Jim: I had no reason to even interrupt or interject quite honestly Than. That was awesome. Like that's exactly the kind of response I would expect from somebody at your level, and that is just great. The MLS it doesn't cost any money to work the MLS, right? Anybody could do that.

Of all the guys I've interviewed, I was very curious to get your specific answer because most guys have not said the MLS quite frankly. I know there's a great opportunity there. Me being an agent first I'm still licensed; I just know that there's an awesome opportunity in the MLS. I was just letting you run with it because that just like a perfect ... I could have scripted that answer; it was so perfect, so thank you for that.

Than: Oh I appreciate yeah. Not to say that ... Everyone who may have answered differently there's always niches and unique opportunities. I like to go where there's going to be plenty of opportunity. That's why I really truly believe in the MLS. I think most of the investors that we coach and work with over the years; I would say at least half their business is being generated off the MLS.

Then the other half is generated from ... This is a generalization but I would say most successful investors buy a certain percentage of their properties off the MLS. They may do everything from direct mail to online marketing to banner signs to ... All the other forms of marketing make up the other 50% because if the majority of properties are being sold in a market on the MLS, there's going to be opportunities there and they're going to go to certain investors who really take the time to build strong relationships with the agents and so-

Jim: Acting fast like you said. I'm one of your students, I don't know if people know that but you're one of my original mentors in the real estate investing business. I get 80% of my deals still to this day from the MLS. I've learned to work it well from stuff you guys taught me originally, and I still work it well today. I had an understanding of it because I was an agent, but really figuring out how to work it, it all really comes down to communication. Just properly communicating with these agents like you said. It's crazy but it's true if you act ...

There are more deals than the average investor will need in the MLS forever. That could be your only deal source quite frankly. I would think a guy looking to do one or two deals a month; most MLSs will provide that if you work it right.

Than: Absolutely. We make about 15 offers on the MLS to get one. We track our metrics pretty religiously. We'll track every single offer that goes out of our office every single week to get averages. We know if our average is going up or going down, but historically it's been about 15 offers to get one deal. It's a numbers game in essence but that's no different than any other form of marketing. You're going to have to put a lot of offers out there to get one accepted. That's what we found historically to be true for us.

Jim: Okay, so about 10% of the offers roughly are what you're getting on the MLS it sounds like?

Than: Yeah, one out of 15 is very consistent for what we do. We'll talk to 15 agents. We'll make those offers. When I say offers that's either a verbal offer or a written offer; one of the two. Most of the time it's written, but occasionally ... We'll chock it up as an offer if we get in communication with the agent.

We take a look at the property, we'll estimate the repair cost to the after-repair value of the property. Then we'll either make a verbal or a written offer. That's how we track it. 15 either verbal or written offers to get one deal. We may put two on a contract. One ends up being a short sale if the bank doesn't necessarily negotiate low enough, and we'll get one out of 15. We may have more under contract than one out of.

We may get one or two under contract out of 15 and end up closing on one. Mostly, the reason we would close on less is we may be negotiating a short sell or the bank isn't willing to accept our offer so if you look at percentages, it's somewhere around 7%, one out of 15 of our offers is getting accepted.

Jim: 7%. That's about ... Any kind of marketing we're doing, whether it's the MLS or doing direct mail, the majority of properties we come across are not going to meet our requirements. They're just not. It's just ... I know you said a lot of people say it's no big deal to MLS because there is such a high number to come in there, but there are good deals. You have to sift through the bad ones, just like any kind of marketing we do. I couldn't agree more.

Than: Definitely. It should be part of every investor's acquisition process. Whether it's a big part or a small part, it will play a part in what you do if you're going to have long-term success in a market. It will definitely play a part, it will be one of your acquisition strategies, it could be the main one, it could be secondary compared to other marketing campaigns, but it's definitely going to be one of the strategies you use.

Than's Productivity Tip:

I do two things that I've done for the past 10 years that are very simple and it doesn't have to be really complicated to be extremely effective for you. I set weekly goals and I set them every Sunday evening. I spend 15 minutes setting goals on a weekly basis and I've done that for the past 10 years and it's been a success habit that has been very effective for myself.

I find that daily goals, I find to be too frequent and you won't consistently follow through. Then, yearly goals, I think, are just too big. I found weekly goals to be a nice cross section. I can look back each Sunday and say, "How productive was I?" I try to hit 80%. If I hit too few, then my goals are too aggressive. If I hit 100%, then I'm probably not setting big enough goals for the week. I try to hit somewhere in that 80% range.

The other thing that I do is at the end of the day, I spend five minutes cleaning my office. Papers stack up, books stack up, and things stack up. If you just spend five minutes before you rush out of the office, whether that's your home office or your regular office, you'll feel ... You'll have such a sense of relief when you come back in the next morning because things are organized and you're ready to attack, as opposed to walking in your office and going, "Oh, geez, things are such a mess."

I found those two habits to be very, very helpful for my own productivity.

For more information on Than's company

visit: www.FortuneBuilders.com

Doug Clark

Doug is from Spike TV's "Flip Men." You might think we see him on TV, that it all came easy for Doug, but you might be happy to find out that he started his Real Estate investment career out like many of you, with no many and no credit.

He had a job that paid him less than $17,000 a year. You might be doing better than Doug was when he started out. He needed to find a way to support his family and he decided to learn real estate investing. In the last 10 years, he had personally flipped over 1,000 houses totaling over $50 million in sales. He had successfully kept in touch with Hollywood, which is how he became the star of "Flip Men" on Spike TV, as well as "Big Money" on ABC.

Now, Doug's passion is real estate investing. He's developing live wealth events and seminars to teach others the same techniques that have proven successful on his international TV shows.

Doug's Answer:

That's a great question. I would actually focus on the same things I had to focus on when I had no experience, no money and no credit. Those things were wholesaling and purchasing properties, what's called "subject to." I'll tell about that in a second, but at the time, it's important for me to tell you that I was under a mountain of debt. I had about $100,000 in school loans to become an airline pilot. I finally got a job that was paying me less than $17,000 a year.

In fact, the people that flew with, all qualified for food stamps and actually used them and I understood it completely. It was a horrible time. I actually was commuting 40 hours a week and then I was working my job about 60 hours a week to make that little money to barely be able to pay my school loan, let alone any housing expenses or food or whatever.

It was a very difficult time and I knew I had to do something different. In my private life, me and my wife were high school sweethearts and really wanted to have children and for years and years, tried every method with every doctor to get pregnant and it just wasn't happening. I remember we went to the doctor one day and he said, "Man, you need to do In Vitro."

I didn't even know what it meant, but as I learned, it was about $20,000. If you do In Vitro and you don't get a baby, now you're out $20,000 and you still don't have a baby. It's a very difficult thing for someone who didn't even make that much in a year, plus I owed 5 times that on school loans to become a pilot. It was a difficult thing. Luckily, I found real estate and it changed everything for me.

My first few deals were wholesale deals. I had made enough money to do the In Vitro, continued on. Unfortunately, the In Vitro did not work. Now, I had to step it up. Make another $20,000 grand, pay for it again and boom, there we were.

Now, at that point, I was flying as much as I could in the middle of the night, making pennies. The only thing I knew about real estate, prior to starting it, was I got paid a little bit of money to fly over it. That was my combined experience.

What I did is I learned that if I could get good and focused on finding properties and not funding them ... Because I had really no means to fund them. If I could get good at finding them ... I enjoyed that part. I realized that no good deals will ever go unfunded. I went to work and I started buying properties, "subject to," which is a way that I could do it for zero money, out of pocket.

That strategy is simple. As I'm finding motivated sellers, I'm simply asking them to keep the current financing in place. If I went to somebody and I was going to purchase their house, we write up a contract and it simply says the funding is subject to the existing mortgage, if there is one.

That way, they can transfer the house over to me. We can sit down a title company, do it in a matter of minutes and I don't have to go. I don't have to qualify for a loan. I don't have to have financing in place. I partnered with a lot of people to get their house sold. I purchased a lot of houses that way. In fact, 23 out of 25 of my first rental properties, I bought subject to. It was a way for me to build a rental portfolio, as well as flipping and reselling the properties. For me, that strategy along with wholesaling.

Now, some of these, I would be under contract. I didn't have the means or the education or the background to fix the property. I'd simply wholesale it, or I would go get a property under contract and then sell that contract or sell the LLC I played under or go on title with the new buyer to secure that position. Those are a couple of ways that I started out, with absolutely no background, no credit, no experience and no money.

Jim: Let me ask you about "subject to." You said, subject to the existing mortgage or whatever their current financing is on that. That's like no money out of your pocket at all. That's a way you were buying things, like literally; you said 23 of your first 25 rental properties? It was no money out of your own pocket?

Doug: Correct. Correct. Some of them required a little bit of money. Often, I would pay something, just to solidify the contract. I would pay $100 at closing, just to make sure there was some transfer of money for services. One of the funniest ones was I was at the closing document table and the guy said, "What I want is a carton of cigarettes."

I said, "A carton? That's like a rectangular box or something. Right?" He says, "Yeah." I said, "Hold on a sec." I had one of the assistants at the title company run down to like 7-11, buy him a packet of cigarettes and that's literally what we put on the contract and that's what he wanted for the transfer of his house. It was

	definitely something with very little or zero money out of pocket.
Jim:	Wow. That's awesome. When you were selling the rights to the contract, you mentioned something about putting an LLC. Can you clarify that? You were signing beneficial rights from the LLC? That's kind of an advanced strategy.
Doug:	It's definitely a strategy that some people I've taught do. I've done a little bit. Typically, I don't anymore, but a lot of people do… It's a little bit of extra work sometimes to set up an LLC to do that, but there is ways that will go around some title seasoning laws and things like that.
	There are some advantages to it. I rarely use it myself, but sometimes in the beginning, it was something I had to explore. Honestly, to set up a company, it's only a few hundred bucks. It's definitely a strategy that people should at least know about.
Jim:	Yeah. Correct. Are you still doing "subject to" today? I know you said that's where you'd start back over again. Are you still doing "subject to" deals today?

Doug: Yep. I do. A lot of it is obviously working with my students and helping them learn that. It's interesting because I've had to be a pioneer in this business, because I'd literally, I didn't have this education. I didn't know any of this stuff. I just kept showing up every single day at every property for sale, every foreclosure auction, every single thing every day and learning how this works and other strategies. Where does the money go and how does this thing actually unfold? I've come up with a lot of things that most people don't understand.

Even very, very seasoned big time investors, they don't even know what buying subject to is. Some title companies don't really understand it. I've even heard some agents say, "Well, there's actually a due-on-sale clause in every mortgage, so you can't do it."

Well, that's true. There is a due-on-sale clause in every mortgage. What it says is essentially, if you transfer the title of the house and the bank finds out, they have the right to call the note due. It's the same. It's no different if you transfer it into your own trust or anything like that, or your own LLC. People do it all the time and don't think twice, that's one of the things people flag, saying, "You shouldn't do this." Well, they didn't really read the due-on-sale clause and I've never, ever had one called due, nor do I know any investor that ever has.

Jim: Gotcha. I see. Well, you've mentioned real estate agents and what a lot of people don't realize is real estate agents don't have a place in most real estate investing transactions and they think a lot of what we do, especially in the wholesale world, subject to, either is fraudulent in some way, which it's not. That's why agents ... I'm a licensed agent in Illinois, so I can say that, but speaking from experience, agents don't really have a place, in most deals that we do. Especially subject to and wholesaling deals. Do you agree there?

Doug: Yeah. I would agree. I think ... agents play a certain role. For a lot of new investors, they need access to multiple listing service data. They need someone that can at least say, "Hey, this is the sales history of the house," or, "This is what's going on the street."

I believe it's a good idea to make a friend or someone who is an agent to help you with some of that important information. Now, do you have to be agent? Do you have an agent for most of these transactions? Absolutely not.

In fact, people assume all the time that I'm a licensed agent or licensed contractor or any of that. I don't have any of those licenses. I've never held them. I never will. It's not important to me. I tell people I have one license. It's not even that important. It's a driver's license.

Jim: Right. A lot of my student and guys I've met over the years, they typically don't want to be licensed. They're worried about it, which I get. They pay for it. They pay agents like $500 or $1,000 year for the year's access. It's obviously the cost of doing business. We need agents in the real estate investing world too. Field agents make great MLS bird dogs. I know a lot of guys that pay for that access, a $1,000 for the year and it's well worth it, or you get an agent on your team.

Your real estate investment team and you find your access that way. Let me ask you about marketing. You said you would do subject to, you would do wholesaling. What about marketing? How would you go about finding a deal? I know you said you went to auctions and you went everywhere you could that was doing real estate stuff. Where would you look for deals and where would you market for deals now? Fund for limits.

Doug: Sure. I think there's way to play that smart. Everyone knows a lot of these traditional places, right? Obviously, any kind of foreclosure auctions there sells online auctions, MLS. Those are all pools that you know about. What I did a while back is said, you know what? How do I find more motivated sellers? How do I work smarter?

What I started realizing is a couple of things. One, using free public data. There's so much information that's on the county reporter's office that people don't understand is out there. For instance, what I did is I started looking at the notice of default. Now, instead of mailing each one or driving all these doors, which could be a hundred plus doors every single day, I didn't do that. I had the simplest strategy. My strategy was this. I looked for any notice in default where the mailing address was different that the property that was having a problem.

In other words, if the NOD is on property A, most people live in property A, but I'm looking for the ones that have a different mailing address, so they don't live in the property that has a problem. Suddenly, you have a situation where they needed to move. It's vacant. Maybe it's a rental property.

My highest target is ones that are out-of-state owners. If somebody was out of state and they have a house that's having an issue in another state, they are highly motivated. I started working with those people and those were a lot of the subject tos that I did, that were very easy. I never met these people. I would have my title company send it to a title company in their state.

They would sit down, get the hundred bucks, sign the stuff, and send it back. It's an excellent, excellent way to do it. Another thing that I found was, again, I scratched my head and I said, "How else can you find some of these properties where you may have a motivated seller?" I started searching city lien. A lot of times, there are city ordinances ... Let's say that you're weeds are too tall. Your grass is too tall. Sometimes it's broken windows. Cars parked out in front. There's a lot of reasons the city can kind of lien or threaten.

I started searching those. I found a lot of people who maybe had this threat that their weeds were too tall. They didn't have the money to take care of it and honestly, here's the interesting thing, is the city didn't really hold you to the fund if you did what they told you.

I would go in, work a deal with these guys, get a property subject to, and then I would simply mow the lawn, go to the city and say, "Look. It's beautiful. It's done." They would drop the lien anyways. It wasn't even something that I ever ended up paying.

Jim: Wow. Sort of an interesting way to get somebody to raise their hand, if you will. Even look for the liens in the village. That's a great little tip there. That's free. Right? All of that is public records stuff. It takes some time but it doesn't take much money. You just got to know where to look. The public records, for everybody listening, if you don't know, they're free.

You can walk into your county assessor's office and those records that are tax records are public record. Anybody can look through them. Anybody. If that's what you're referring to. Then there's obviously public record companies that produce that information, but if you're limited on money, those are going to cost money, you can walk in, pull these records for yourself. Correct?

Doug: Absolutely. I tell my students ... a lot of them get a little frustrated or say, "How can I find these deals? How can I find cash buyers? I'm finally getting us some properties. How do I find cash buyers?" I'm like, are you kidding me? Cash buyers are a matter of record. You can pull it up right there.

I say, "Look, if you don't know how to do it, then call a title company and in the time that it would take you to drink a cup of coffee and have a free cookie at the title company, they can pump out the list and give it to you for free as well. More likely, they're going to put you on a daily mailing list for free. There's either a title company or walk into the county recorder itself and have documentation. It's free. It's there. You don't have to guess who is buying the cash in your area. Its matter of public record and it's right there in front of you.

Doug's Productivity Tip:

You bet. One thing I use is called a T4. These are the key four things, that if I do this week, I will get paid the quickest. What I do every Sunday night or Monday morning is I sit down and I take four sticky notes out and I write down what that key number one is. I write down what it is and I write the who, what, where, when of the exact day, what I need to do, who I need to call to get that objective completed.

These are the just four things in a week that are each different sticky notes, that are right in front of me, that I committed, I will do these four things, this week, it's a short term goal, and these are the quickest things I can do to get paid.

I always focus them on the quickest way to get paid. Some of that ... Again, it depends on me or my student or where we're at that week, as far as some of them will create dollars that week, other ones are just going to create "What's the smartest thing I can do to get paid next week or next month?" It's really the four most important things this week, that I need to accomplish above all else to make sure that I am bringing money in.

For more information on Doug's company

and his live training events visit:

www.Clarkedu.com

CHIEF DENNEY

Chief Denny, from the TV show "Flipping San Diego." Chief has been a real estate investor since his early 20s, and this guy has done deals all over the country. He has done thousands of deals at this point, he stopped keeping count. Hopefully, you can get to a point in your career where you can stop keeping count of how many deals you've done. This guy has done stuff all over the real estate investing business; he's a real estate junkie. We're talking a guy that earns over seven figures a year, but he's a real family man. He loves being a dad. He has a degree in architecture, but he's a big time real estate investor. He's in the San Diego market. He also does a lot of private money lending, so if you're in that area, you might want to look him up for private lending needs. This is a guy who's been all over the real estate market for a long time, and done very well.

Chief's Answer:

That's a great question. You know, I got started with nothing, so it's not too horribly difficult to answer. The first thing I would work on, is finding money. It sounds crazy, because everyone's looking for a strategy, you know, "Should I be a wholesaler? Should I bird dog?" Should I do assignment of contracts? Should I find a fix and flip, where I can earn a few bucks, maybe joint venture with someone?" Those are all really great tools, and they all work. But one of the things that I've learned, is he who has the money, makes the rules. He who has the money, has opportunity. I've always told people, and it's probably the only quote I've ever been quoted on is, "All good deals find money, and money finds good deals, and all good deals get done." One of the things is, if you realize that people that have means, people that have money, they're always looking for opportunity. They're looking for a way to make their money grow.

Then there are people that are out there searching for deals. I'd rather be the person that has the money. The deals are coming to me, and I can say yes or no. It sounds a bit weird, because when we talk about maybe real estate flipping, and things like that, we want to just dive right into, you know, "Go find a deal, so I can…" Then go shake the trees for money. But real money, not just grandma and grandpa, who can throw you a few bucks, and help you do your first deal. But someone who can really fund your multiple deals, can sit there and fund five, ten, fifteen deals a year for you, or five, ten, fifteen deals a month for you, they can smell (laughs) everything that you're afraid of. When someone's brand new, they're not quite sure of themselves. They're not quite sure of the numbers. They have some reservations. It can be intimidating. So, what happens is, you tend to get the short end of the stick. You tend to come from a position of weakness. So, I've always looked at, and I've always told people, "Look, the first order of business, is to really know what you're talking about."

It doesn't mean you've had to do a deal, doesn't mean you experientially know what you're talking about, but you really have to read up, study. Obviously, take a course. Anything you can do to speak intelligently to it, and then go look for the money, because money is hungry. Right now, there's more money on the sidelines. Regardless of where the economy is, up, down, sideways, there's always more money in the sidelines looking for opportunity. If you can align yourself with the money, you don't even have to have a deal. The first thing I would do is, I would learn how to, let's say we're going to talk about flipping homes, I would learn how to flip a home. I would learn how to package, packaging, huge. Most people just throw junk into some one page flyer, which is nonsense. If you're trying to get me to write a check for half a million bucks, or if you're trying to get me to write a check for fifty thousand bucks, if you can't professionally package it, and give it to me I have no interest in talking to you, or looking at your deal, because you haven't taken the time to be professional at your end.

You're asking me for money? Wow me. Convince me. Blow me away. Show me that you know what you're doing. Learning how to package a deal, which means numbers, and pictures, and great stuff like that, and then, even if you haven't done the deal, you could show me other people's deals. You could show me someone else that has a successful deal. "Here's a deal I was looking at. I'm new to this. I've got someone holding my hand. I've got a business partner, where I do the hard work, where I look for stuff, and he's kind of holding my hand as I get into this industry. What I'm looking for, is I'm looking for a capital partner to financially support me. Here's the deal I tried to buy. I couldn't buy it, but I want to share with you what my competition's doing. What's available in our own backyard? What kind of profit there is to be made in this business?"

It's maybe a different answer than what you're looking for, but if you have money, you have confidence. If you have fifty thousand.

Jim: It's no different than what I'm looking for, that's great. Most people do look for the deal first, and so this is a different approach. The way most people go into the business, is they try to find a deal, and then they scatter with what to do, like, "Oh my God, do I close on it myself? Where do I find the money? Do I wholesale it? What do I do now?" They don't have an exit strategy, they just find a property and then half the time they have to back out of it, because they don't know what to do with it. Or they have no money to buy it.

Doug: Right. As you get closer to that, let's say you have a two week due diligence period, you got two weeks to figure out if your comps are right. You've got two weeks to get the contract in, to figure out how much it's going to cost to fix, you've got two weeks to find the dough. All of sudden, day one, you're confident, day two, you're confident, day three...a little chink in the armor. But, you come down to day ten, you're freaking out. "Where am I going to find the money?" I know this, because that's how I got started. I had many deals and I was always scrambling for money. When you're scrambling for money...They always say never sell when you're hungry, only sell when you're full. Because when you're hungry, people can see the desperation. They can sense that. Day thirteen, you got twenty-four hours to close a deal so you can go make twenty-five grand, or fifty grand, or a hundred and fifty grand, and you're freaking out. Now you make bad business decisions. You get in bed with the wrong business partners, who might steal a deal from you. You're just ill prepared.

It makes much more sense, to pretend. Have a deal packaged, you're not doing this deal, it could have been a deal that was done last week, last month, but you're demonstrating what is in the marketplace. You're demonstrating your ability to find these deals. You're demonstrating that, "You know what? I'm a source of opportunity. Let me show it to you. Let me prove to you it works." Then you find your capital partners. And when you find your capital partners, now you're coming from a position of strength. Here's what's very interesting, people in San Diego know that I fund deals. My competition. So I'm out there building, we're doing land development, we're building projects in the housing tracts, and we flip too. I think we've got seventeen homes we're flipping this month. What happens is, my competition. Someone like Than, he's in our backyard her in San Diego. Maybe he's got a deal. He outbid me and he got it. He was successful. Well, that's probably a bad example to use. Let's just pick someone that's not known.

A buddy of mine, Mark...Let me rewind. So, my buddy Mark, this is true, two weeks ago, Mark found a place in Pacific Beach. He needed a million two to do this deal, and he didn't have it. So, who'd he call? He called me. Well guess what? He wouldn't have called me if he didn't know I could fund the deal. What's interesting, is by being on the money side of the equation, and it's not all my money, it's investor money too, so it's me and my investors. What happens is now deals come to me. I'm not looking for them. They come to me, because people will always gravitate to where the money is. So, if you're new to this business, again, you don't have to have money to find money. If you're new to this business, aligning yourself with people that have fat checkbooks is a much easier way to start this business. Deal flow, opportunity will come much faster if they know you can write a check. When I say, "You write a check." Obviously, we know, we always work with our investors. You and I can write a check, but we also have our investors who can write a check too. If I were starting all over again, instead of chasing deals, I'd chase money.

Jim: Get yourself aligned with the right people. I don't want to use, "Fake it til you make it," but at the beginning, you got to do that sometimes. You got to go learn the business, use other people's wins as, "Hey, this is what's going on in our market." Where do you go to look for the money? To find a guy like you in your market, obviously, they're going to know now. If they didn't know you did, you lend money in the San Diego market, but where would you go to start out? Would you start out the REIAs? Where would you go to try to find money initially?

Doug: Again, I'm probably a little different. I tell people to go to REIAs, REIAs a good place. The challenge with REIAs is, I break life always into three segments on everything, so we'll break the REIA into three sections. Thirty-three percent of the people, so a third of the people, are the real deal. A third of the people are there just like you, someone brand new, learning as well, so that's not going to be a lot of benefit. And a third of the people are just habitual REIA attenders. How do you, when you're new, differentiate the right third? The challenge with REIA is a lot of people will make grand promises; they'll fund deals, blah, blah, blah, blah, blah. When they really can't. Then again, you've got fourteen day due diligence, day thirteen, the person you thought, and believed in to fund your deal, actually walks out of the deal, and now, you got egg on your face, because you implicitly trusted someone. REIA is a good place to go. Great information. What you can do is you can pull from title companies. Find out who the players are in town. Title companies, title rep, will tell you who the players are, whose buying volume.

You can find out from the REIAs, you can look at the message boards, you can see who the players are. You can talk to the REIA, and people know names in towns, but title's a good source of it. You can talk to hard moneylenders, private moneylenders. They obviously work with a lot of flippers. They know. You can go down to the auctions. Most states, when you go down to a trustee sale auction, or a foreclosure auction, the real ones. That's all cash on the barrelhead in most states. These aren't wishy-washy people. The kind that can show up, and buy eleven homes at half a million dollars a throw. I mean, he's got deep pockets. That's a great source to find out who the players are. What I like about that is, you know they're looking for deals. You know they have money, and they've got a history, a track record. What's great is, one, you can learn from them. Two, you can feed deals to them. Three, if you got a deal, that makes financial sense; guess what, they're used to writing checks. So, either they write a check, you can joint venture with them. You could wholesale a deal to them. They can fund your deal for you as a capital partner. So, you've opened up multiple doors.

Jim: This is all free stuff too. It takes a little leg work, obviously, to go to the title company, to go to the auction, to see who the real players are. Even go to the RIA. You could always ask the REIA, the guy who organizes, or runs the REIA, he will always know who that third of the room is that's real players, and he will tell you...

Doug: Absolutely.

Jim: You can and should ask the guy who's running the REIA who to talk to, because he'll point you in the right direction. These are all free, right. These are all free, going to find people who can fund your deals.

Doug: absolutely. You brought up a really, really good point. Here's what's important, making sure you're dealing with real people. We know, in any industry, there are a lot of people that aren't real. There's a lot of talkers, is what I call them, versus doers. What's nice, to your point, is going up to the president of the RIA, the person that's hosting the RIA, and asking them who the doers are. That saves so much time. It allows you to accelerate to the front of the pack immediately.

Chief's Productivity Tip:

I'm anal about planning. I'm a huge planner. I have a quote, that I write, and it's on my planner every day, and it says, "I choose to live my life by my design." I don't believe you can just successfully walk through life, and just be blessed with every gift and reward you want. I think God will meet you half way. You got to put in the blood, sweat, and tears. I use a Franklin planner, which sounds, probably archaic, because most people now use smart phones, and all this other stuff, but I'm fifty, so I still scribble with a pencil in my hand. But I love a planner; because I can sit down, get my thoughts out there. They have their own planning system, the Franklin planning, which I think everything is derived from that, but it's just basically ABC. A is what's my priority, B, what's important, C, what can be pushed off til whenever. Then number them, one, two, and three. I really, seriously look at what I'm trying to accomplish, this year, this month, this week, and then today. Every night, at the end of the day, I review my day. What did I get done? What did I not get done? Do I need to spend more time with my kids? Am I out of balance? We're always out of balance, but...Balance is kind of bunk, really.

Jim: Shifting the balance from time to time is helpful.

Doug: Yeah. Exactly. So, when I'm watching my son play hockey, I don't answer the phone. I'm fully focused on his hockey. When I'm at my daughter's event in volleyball, I'm there. I'm not talking business, that's where I'm at. But likewise, when I'm at my desk, and I'm working, my kids know that, hey, "I'm working." I'm not interrupted. I plan my day in the morning. I review it at night, and time blocking. Time blocking is huge. Certain times of the day are dedicated to certain activities. From 6:30 to 7:30, it's kid time. From 7:45 to 9:00, it's exercise gym time, and I'm unavailable. From 9:00 to 5:00, it's work. That's what I'm doing. I'm rocking and rolling. Then, it's family time. Certain days are different. So what happens, I know that every Thursday, I'm not at the desk, I'm out of the office on Thursdays, because I'm in the field looking at all our different projects. That's Thursday. I know Fridays is accounting time, sitting down and making sure payroll, and accounts receivable, and all that fun stuff's being done. I think people call it chunking, time chunking, I call it time blocking.

Then I have clarity of purpose. If you're new to this business, you got to be clear, what to do Monday, what to do Tuesday, what to do Wednesday. You need to be clear what you do in the morning, and what you do in the evening. If you're clear, that way you can avoid all the outside interruptions. You got to break the bad habits of lollygagging, being lazy, not being focused. When you're new to this business, you've got to be laser focused. The whole new thing. There's got to be time dedicated to learn, there's got to be time dedicated to meet new people. There's got to be time dedicated to learning the skills. Let me rewind with something. The number one thing you can do in this business, other than find money, so I'll say the number two thing, is to write lots and lots and lots and lots of offers. No offers equals no money. Lots of offers equals lots of money. I'm always blown away. People say, "Oh, it's not working for me." "How many offers did you write? None. Duh." The more offers you write,

	the more money you're going to make. We bang out a hundred offers a month easily.
Jim:	A lot of new students come to me, and they say, "I wrote seven offers, and I didn't get one of them." I say, "Write a hundred more, and then call me back. If we have a problem then, maybe we have to adjust something. But you're not even close."
Doug:	Yep exactly, it's a numbers game. And at the end of the day, here's what's great about this business. You can make a ridiculous amount of money. Whatever that means to someone. I make seven figures a year. People don't have to make seven figures a year. For many people, to make an extra forty, or fifty thousand dollars a year, is a huge homerun. For other people, they want to make an extra forty, fifty thousand a month. Okay, that's fine. For some people, they want to make forty, fifty thousand every two weeks. What's nice is this business, you can check the box to yes on all those figures. Forty a year, forty a month, or forty a week. This business lets you do it. You just have to work your butt off. For forty thousand dollars a year, some people

work real hard, for a few million dollars a year, willing to work very hard. I can't think of another industry that allows us to do this, that's why I love, I mean, I love this business.

Jim: I couldn't agree more. Set your goal, reverse engineer it, figure out what you got to do to reach your income goal, and that's where you should start with anything really, but especially getting in the real estate business. Set a goal. Most people, I think, get into this business and they go "Hope to do a deal, and hope to make forty grand extra. Maybe can I do two deals this year?" Not that there's anything wrong with making an extra eighty grand, because, that's great. But, you should be setting a goal and working backwards, and figuring out what you have to do to get that into place. And I think, like you said at the beginning, getting your money lined up, so if you want to make four hundred grand a year, well in order to do that, you have to set up a lot of money to buy the deals that are going to help you make four hundred grand a year. It's just putting everything in perspective, and getting all your ducks in a row, and treating this like a business that you can make millions of dollars at, because you can. I just think too many people don't get the right education.

Doug: Yeah. And that's why I think that I'm probably a little different than saying hey "you should wholesale your first deal, so you can go pinch a quick fifteen, twenty grand, or five grand, or whatever." We just got an offer accepted today, the house, we're in it at two point three million dollars. You can't do those deals if you don't have money lined up. My exit, I'll have two hundred grand into it, so I'll be in it for two point three, plus another two hundred grand, so two point five million. Throw another hundred grand in there for taxes, insurance, and holding costs, so I'll be in it for two point six. My exit on this place, because this will be six months from check to check, is three point six. So, take out some closing costs, it's a high six figure net, net, net profit. Can't do deals like that if you don't have the capital behind you. Obviously, if you're starting, you're probably not chasing a two million dollar deal; you're probably chasing a twenty thousand dollar deal, a hundred and twenty thousand dollar deal. The process is exactly the same. If you have that money behind you, supporting you, deal flow, the doors open, and deals come your way. Getting back to square one, I'm really big on focus on finding the money. When you have the money, all good deals find money, money finds good deals, and all good deals get done.

For more info about Chief and his company visit: http://chiefpropertyventures.com

Chief has a very small 1 on 1 coaching group that he offers. He also lends money to those students that are in his market in Southern CA.

Chief is also one of the largest private money lenders in Southern California.

For more info on that email him at:

info@chiefpropertyventures.com

Kent Clothier

Kent is founder of, get this, he's founder and CEO of several companies, Real Estate Worldwide, 1-800 Sell Now, Find Cash Buyers Now, Find Private Lenders Now, Find Motivated Sellers Now. Kent's primary focus is in the real estate investing, marketing, and education spaces.

This guy is a serial entrepreneur that, since age 17 has started over eleven multimillion-dollar organizations. One of them reaching, get this, one point seven billion, with a B, in annual sales. Although Kent has had great success in business, his biggest accomplishment is his family. He lives with his wife Seema and their three kids in beautiful La Jolla California.

Kent's Answer:

Good question. There's no doubt that what we would focus on is exactly what we focus on today, that is wholesaling. Where most people think of wholesaling in the traditional sense of it's a low barrier of entry, it's a very easy way to get involved in real estate, you don't have to know a lot, you don't have to a ton of knowledge, and you can get in and out of a deal very, very quickly, and actually make a considerable amount of money for the amount of effort.

Wholesale fees can go from anywhere from a thousand dollars to, depending on the market, they can be fifty thousand dollars. There's no doubt that would be the strategy, if I'm starting all over again, that we would gravitate to immediately. With a twist, because, answering the second part of your question, Jim, what has made us traditionally so successful in our real estate business has been the simple fact that we do wholesaling considerably different.

We actually treat it like a business as opposed to what most investors, especially brand new investors when they get involved they treat it almost like a hobby, they're doing it trying to make a few bucks and get going. This is a big business for us. We flip six hundred properties a year doing exactly what I'm about to share with you right now. It's called reverse wholesaling. You mentioned a company that we started and ultimately grew to one point seven billion dollars.

The way we did that was in the grocery industry, not the real estate industry. We did it using a method called reverse wholesaling. Basically, to sum it all up you start with the end in mind, you start with the buyers, you start with the people that have the money, you start with the people that have the motivation and the desire, you really work closely with them to figure out exactly what it is that they want, you build and nurture those relationships, then you turn and around and effectively go shopping with their money.

That is still exactly what we do inside of our real estate business today. It is the exact same strategy I would use. We market heavily to cash buyers. In today's market they make up 40, 50% of the market depending on where you are. These people have money, they have means, they have motivation, and they're actively doing it right now so they don't need financing. They don't bring the headaches, they don't bring the middle men, and they don't bring any of that nonsense that traditionally makes real estate, brings out the brain damage to the equation.

Why would you not focus on those people, they're the path of least resistance? We focus on those people, we market to them heavily. We use our own databases to get them to engage us directly, call us, and then we nurture those relationships. We find out exactly what it is that they want to buy, how much they're willing to pay, what neighborhoods they want to buy their properties in, and then we go get it.

It becomes infinitely easier to wholesale a house to somebody, to sell somebody a house if you know exactly what they're willing to pay, exactly what neighborhoods they want to buy in, exactly what the property looks like. When you have all of that information and you're not guessing, this business becomes so much easier. If I had to start all over today, I would go out right now and I would scrape together whatever I had to scrape together to get access to this database of cash buyers.

If I couldn't scrape anything together, then I would get down into the public courthouses, the County Recording Clerk's office and find people there, in the transactions. In the recorded deeds from the previous week I would find everybody that bought a house last month that didn't record a mortgage, because if they didn't record a mortgage and they bought a house that's a cash buyer. I would actively-

Jim: What people listening may not know is that anybody ... You can use your Find Cash Buyers Now, but anybody in any county recording office, you can walk in there and go through, that's public records so you can go through there. It's a lot of time, it's extremely time consuming, but if you don't have any money, you can walk up to your county assessor's office and do it for free. It just takes some time, right?

Kent: That's exactly right. That's exactly how we got started. We automated this whole process because, it comes back to one of the very first things I said, we started treating this like a business. To your point, we weren't willing to invest all that time and effort in a manual process. We figured out a way to automate it, but if you don't have access, you march down there; you go sit there and park it there for hours on end, whatever it takes. This is exactly how we got started.

Whatever it takes to locate and identify the people that are paying cash because cash investors, cash buyers are investors. They buy multiple properties. Anybody who pays cash for a property, they're not buying their primary residence, they're investors, they're buying it with a purpose, with a mission. They're trying to get a return so this is a really good candidate. Somebody who, if you could focus a lot of attention on them, you'd sell them multiple properties.

They're more than willing, just like any of us would be. They're more than willing that, if somebody comes to them and says "Hey, let me do all the work. Let me go find the properties and bring them to you at the price you want to pay," they're more than willing to day that. Who wouldn't be? Because they don't have to do anything. They're getting served up properties on a silver platter. You are taking on that responsibility.

You go and engage these cash buyers, you write all their information down, you do whatever you've got to do, do a little Facebook, whatever. You've got to track them down, pick up the phone, call them, mail them, get them on the phone, engage them, build a relationship with them, and be very intentional with what you're trying to do. In other words, literally focus on trying to help them to do what they're trying to do, that's buy more properties, then you have your marching orders.

I can assure you it gets infinitely easier, as I just said, to go find property when you know exactly what you're looking for. The big mistake brand new investors make today, and the thing that's the most overwhelming to them and where they get paralyzed, is they don't know how to find a good deal and quite frankly don't know if it is a good deal because what they're taught to do is run up and down the streets, knock on doors, do all this guerrilla type marketing, mail these lists.

Then if somebody picks up the phone and calls them and says, "Yeah, I'll sell you my house," "What price do I buy it for? Who am I going to sell it to? How do I know if it's a good deal?" When you do it the way I'm telling you to do it, all that goes out the window because you're only looking for properties in the very areas you know your cash buyers want to buy, you're only buying properties at prices that you know your cash buyers are willing to pay from you.

The cash buyer wants to pay you two hundred thousand dollars and you want to make ten grand, the most you can pay is one ninety, any way, shape, or form, that's the way it is. All the speculation and all the guessing and all the sleepless nights and all the twisted up, knotted stomachs, "Did I make a good deal or not a good deal?", all that goes out the door.

You know what they're willing to pay, you know where they want to buy it, you go get it, then you put the property under contract, quickly assign your contract to the buyer and you're in and out. It doesn't get any easier than that. That becomes a system. People ask me a lot about how you do multiple deals. Here's the big piece of advice, get out of the transaction business and get in the client business and the relationship business. Build relationships with cash buyers and you've got a business. If you sit there and chase money and you go from deal to deal to deal, you've got a job.

Jim: Right, like you said a lot of new investors are looking for the one bonus, could I do a deal this month or in the next couple months and get one quick, little bonus check. It's a hobby. It's not a business. Reverse wholesaling, essentially you reversed engineered the entire business, which is what you should do with any business. You start with the end in mind, work your way backwards, and you have yourself a business plan. Right?

Kent: That's exactly right. Your clients will tell you everything that you want to know about doing business with them. It's truly, as far as I'm concerned, it's the lowest common denominator. This is as easy and as straightforward as you can possibly make it for the novice to get in business. It's about as easy and straightforward as you can make it for the seasoned pro to streamline their business and do a lot more business.

I can definitely tell you, again, people ask me this all the time ... I was twenty-seven years old when we took a company from doing eight hundred million to one point seven billion. What

I just shared with you was the quote, unquote magic formula. You're exactly right, it seems too easy, but the reality of it is that nobody else does this.

Jim: Let me ask about marketing strategy. You have your cash buyer, to find the deals, what marketing strategy would you focus on with limited funds? Obviously you guys have more money than you know what to do with to market. If you were starting out again, how would you find deals? We know how to find the buyers, what would you do to find deals?

Kent: Again, there's no shortage of people in the market. Imagine this for a second. There's no shortage of people in the market that are looking for the lowest common denominator, meaning that they don't want to work real hard to get paid. There are other wholesalers, there are other bird dogs, and there are certainly other realtors in your market right now that are doing it the hard way.

If somebody picked up the phone to them today and said, "Listen, I have half a million dollars I can spend. I need to buy a property in the next seven days. In fact I need to buy two properties in the next seven days. I need them in Southeast Shelby County; I need them in the Hillsborough neighborhood, three bedroom, two bath, brick homes, that I'm willing to pay two hundred grand for. They have to be able to rent for twenty-two hundred dollars a month. They need a maximum of twenty-five thousand dollars in rehab. The most I can pay for them is a hundred and sixty thousand dollars. I've got cash and I can close in seven days", there's no shortage of people that will take those marching orders and go do all the heavy lifting for you.

The reason they'll do it is because you're now speaking as though you've got the money. The reason you can do that is because you have a cash buyer behind you that is saying, "I'll write the check. Bring me the property at," whatever it is, "a hundred and eighty thousand dollars or a hundred and seventy thousand dollars needing twenty-five thousand dollars rehab that I can rent for twenty-two hundred dollars a month.

Three bedroom, two bath, Hillsborough County, Southeast part of Shelby," whatever.

You're regurgitating back to the market what your cash buyer wants; all you're doing is building in your margin. Once you understand what your cash buyer wants, picking up the phone and calling every wholesaler, every bird dog, and every realtor that works those neighborhoods, and telling them that you are now a cash buyer that wants to buy, and giving them those very specific parameters is exactly what they're looking for because they are used to doing it the other way.

If you're a realtor, you're used to driving people around on Saturday and Sunday, spending time away from your family, rarely making money, and rarely having things that actually pan out. You're doing very few deals a year, if you're just a normal realtor, and it's a hard grind. Suddenly somebody picks up the phone and tells you exactly what they want in the exact neighborhood they want, the exact price they're willing to pay, and that they'll close in seven days. Again, you can say this because your cash buyer has told you the same exact thing. They want to close in seven days.

All you're going to do is assign the contract to them. It's very straightforward. I can prove to you how true this actually is because this is exactly what the hedge funds have done. The hedge funds have stepped into almost every real estate market in the United States. They know nothing about real estate. They're getting better, but when they started they knew nothing. What they do know how to do very, very well is sell money.

If you really boiled it down to the essence of what these hedge funds have done, they walk into a market and they simply say, they'll issue a press release, it'll be on the morning news, the newspaper, whatever, they'll say, "Blackrock is going to invest twenty-five million dollars in single family homes in Shelby County, Tennessee over the next five years. Call Amy at Blackrock at 555 ..." Suddenly Amy's phone is ringing off the hook because every realtor, every wholesaler, every investor is looking at Amy as the one stop shop. They have all the money. They know exactly what they want. Amy can solve all my problems. Let get Amy to tell me exactly what she wants and I'll go get it.

Jim: They might not know real estate, but they know marketing, right?

Kent: You got it. This is all you're doing. This is all I was doing. I literally wouldn't leave the house. I'd go and find the cash buyers, then I'd turn around and I would engage the realtors and investors in the market, tell them exactly what I'm looking for, how much money I can now spend because my cash buyers had told us, and I would sell the money. Money talks. If you can close quick, like you now can when you have these cash buyers, like seven days, and you know exactly what you want, it is amazing how many people will go to work and find everything you ever want.

Jim: Wow. That's awesome. Again, it's a matter of making some phone calls, finding the right people that want to buy, finding the right people that want to sell, and essentially setting up a bunch of bird dogs, wholesalers and realtors and people that work that market already. Have them to the work for you. When you say it that way it seems so easy.

Kent: It really is. Again, I'm not going to sit here and tell you that every realtor you talk to or every cash buyer you talk to is going to be bending over backwards to do business with you. I don't want to give anybody the wrong impressions. The reality of it is that this kind of work makes more sense and is more logical and is a better, streamlined way of setting yourself to do a lot of business versus driving up and down the streets, looking for boarded up houses, laying out [bandit 00:15:56] signs. All of those things work, but you asked me specifically what I would do and what I believe is the easiest and fastest way in any market to make things happen, there it is.

Jim: It's cost effective too. This is phone calls. Everybody has got a phone already.

Kent: They're already doing the work. All you're trying to do is motivate them to do the work for you.

Kent's Productivity Tip:

I'll share a couple with you. I'm a big technology guy. We use a lot of different things in our business to automate and streamline what we do. We use Trello, is a CRM that I've found to be a very good, personal tool. It's a piece of software that allows me to really manage multiple projects. I have a lot of different people working for me; I can keep my eye on the pulse. It's a really interactive way for me to engage my teams. The way we actually manage our internal business, we use a piece of software called Podio which is another great tool for real estate investors on how to really manage your business. It's a free tool that is excellent.

That's T, R, E, L, L, O. They're both free. The other one is Podio, P, O, D, I, O. Again, fantastic tools that we use online. The last one I use that I'm addicted to, as most people that I know who use it are, is Evernote. A lot of ideas, a lot of things going at the same time. Evernote is a really good way for us to keep our arms around multiple things. We've got it setup where all of these tools interact with each other. Those are three things I would share with you, and they're all free.

Kent can be reached at one of many places.

http://www.KentClothier.com

http://www.RealEstateWorldWide.com

1-800-Sell-Now

Find Cash Buyers Now

Find Private Lenders Now

RON LEGRAND

This guy has been around being an entrepreneur for 48 years. He's been doing real estate for 32 of those years from every aspect of it, from commercial development to speaker, author. He's a trainer. He sells information products and he's been in the mortgage lending end of this business. He's done almost 3000 single family deals and his commercial background also includes in nine different states he's done anything from retail to warehouse to residential developments to he's dealt with resort properties. He currently does about 6 to 12 houses every month without using any money or credit, and almost none of his own time with only a staff of two people.

He's an instructor on many subjects from including residential, commercial, private lending, business management, marketing, business growth. He spoke to over 500,000 students around the world. He's spoke on platforms with people from Donald Trump to Robert Kiyosaki to Rudy Giuliani to Jay Leno, Dr. Phil, past presidents, actors, business leaders, just to name a few. When you talk about rock stars in real estate investing, this guy will be in the Hall of Fame.

Ron's Answer:

I would do first what I've been teaching people to do for a lot of years now because the way we do business, it doesn't require money and in fact, if you're using your money, you're doing it incorrectly and it most certainly doesn't require credit. I spank people for using their credit, so I would do what I have been doing for a long time now and that is I'd do the real estate techniques that don't require money or bank loans or risk, for that matter.

A lot of people think that is wholesaling properties, which is actually how I did get started but gosh, I don't wholesale properties anymore. I've found that the other side of the business, the beautiful homes in the beautiful neighborhoods is where the really easy money is and we make that money without...

We don't use banks. We don't use short sales. No contractors. No repairs. No costly entanglements. In fact, we make most of that money by appealing and making it easy for the 80% of the population looking to buy houses that can't qualify for a loan and not catering to the 20% who can qualify for a loan, and we've learned to do all of this without risk and, honestly, we make more money on the big, beautiful, higher end houses than we do on the lower end starter homes.

We are in the terms business, Jim. We work with sellers who will give us terms which means lease option or owner financing and then we offer those terms into the marketplace which attracts our buyers to us and makes it 20 times easier to sell the properties because they have terms. It really is usually just a delayed cash sale. We put them in the house on a lease purchase or with owner financing, and our big payday comes from the down payment we collect from the buyers. When you can allow people to get into a beautiful home and give them time to fix whatever's broke, which could be, I don't know, credit perhaps or perhaps debt ratio is not right or perhaps they're self-employed or whatever.

There's nothing that's broke that can't be fixed with time, so we put them in the house and give them a year, two years, three years, whatever it takes and to help them get cashed out and sometimes it's a permanent deal. We don't ever have to cash them out, so we buy with terms and we sell with terms, therefore making the houses very easy to sell because we're making them easy to buy.

If I lease optioned your house from you, you wouldn't get any money upfront. We just agree when I start making payments, but that same house taken into the marketplace, I would get a nonrefundable option deposit out of my buyer and that's going to start at $5,000 and go up. You know what I learned? I learned that the higher priced properties we deal in, the bigger number up is, which people...

Jim: When you're getting 5,000, what price point is that at? For a nonrefundable deposit, that does seem like a lot.

Ron: I honestly don't even touch a house for 5,000 anymore. I've learned that it's easier to get a person buying a $300,000 house, easier to get $25,000 out of them than it is to get $5,000 out of somebody buying a $100,000 house, so we go into the beautiful neighborhoods where the gorgeous houses are where the people with money but not yet qualified, can't afford to buy, and they have more money to put down. Remember, our compensation comes from that down payment or that deposit, so obviously, the more we can get down, the more we get to keep.

Jim: Got it, so the only compensation you're getting at all is from that nonrefundable deposit at the beginning of a transaction and then you're stepping away from the thing.

Ron: No, no. Not at all. Actually, we work real hard to stay in it. Then we get money upfront, a spread monthly between what we collect and what we pay, and then many times on the backend, there's still equity because we bought the house cheaper than the current market value and, don't forget that values go up. When we buy the house from the seller at a fixed price, that doesn't necessarily mean that we have to fix that price going forward, so we may get the advantage of appreciation if done properly.

We get money on the front end, money monthly, and money on the backend. That's what we call a golden goose. Keep just laying those golden eggs so we get paid many times for doing the job once and again, the higher priced property we work on, the bigger those paydays are.

I'm doing that in the United States of America and Canada. It works anywhere and everywhere we go. As you know, I trained all over the country. The students, I have well over a million students. I don't even know anymore. I quit counting years ago.

There's really not much that we do today anyway. I used to spend a lot of money getting sellers to call me. Today we spend almost none. In fact, I can tell you right now, you could make a very, very high six-figure income if you didn't do anything but call FSBO signs in front of people's houses, for sale by owners, and/or simply follow up on the ads that they run online on the sites like Craigslist.

The key, Jim, is to get all of this other stuff done by other people for very small amounts of money so today, I don't spend ... I promise you I don't spend two or three hours a week max at real estate and neither do my two staff. I have a personal assistant. She doesn't spend 20% of her time in real estate, and then she has a personal assistant that spends about the same. We have a lot of other things going on.

There's only a few things that one must do to make this business work and almost all of that is done by virtual assistants, so we have virtual assistants do all the grunt work, all the work that nobody really wants to do, so that I, as the business owner, can sit back and do the one thing business owners are responsible for doing and that's making decisions. I make very, very few of those. My entire real estate business doing anywhere from 5 to 10 houses a month is all done on autopilot by very, very low, inexpensive labor called virtual assistants and with the help of my assistant or two. In fact, it's rarely anymore do I even go out into the house. It's just something that you can replace yourself to do very quickly.

Jim: It's that automate at this point, so that is incredible.

Ron: It's never been more automated in my 32 years.

Jim: Wow. That is impressive. They're calling the for sale by owners. Obviously anybody can do that, anybody starting out could do that for nothing because Craigslist is free and I'm sure everybody has a cellphone, so is that really one of the best tools right now is to just call the for sale by owners that are out there?

Ron: It's the highest quality FSBO lead there is and that's when a sign is sitting in front of a house.

Jim: That's a great tip coming from Ron LeGrand saying to call the for sale by owners, you would have thought that would be a lead that would be something that might not be worth calling quite honestly because in all the interviews I've done with this, nothing's come up with for sale by owners yet which is surprising, especially when you're saying it's your mainly what you would focus on, so that's really great.

Ron: I am much heavier into the pretty house business than I used to be, but it's been probably three, four years now that we really changed our focus. Look, I've done it all. I've done the wholesales, I've done the rehabbing, I've done the residential, done the commercial as you said, but there's just nothing more easier than finding beautiful homes in beautiful neighborhoods, working with the people who will give us terms which frankly our virtual assistants find out before we even get our hands on that information. They ask them if they had owner finance or lease purchasing. It's a yes or no answer, and would you believe 36% of the FSBO ads and the FSBO signs say yes to terms? 36% say yes to terms.

It's now just a matter of following up and figuring out what terms and going out and getting that agreement and getting it into the marketplace.

Jim: Would you say they're agreeing to terms because they're in a position where it paid off or are they don't know any ... It seems like that's a high offer.

Ron: There are three kinds of properties you'll find. First is over leveraged. We have a system where we make money on houses that are over leveraged now. Secondly is that there's a mortgage on them, but they do have some equity in them, and thirdly, they are free and clear. 34% of the houses in this country are free and clear right now. Those are a gold mine, so we work with all three. We just simply need sellers who will give us terms and then we can offer those terms to our buyer. Sometimes those terms are long term. Never are they less than two years.

Jim: Two years is the least you're going to see?

Ron: Yeah, it's the least I'm going to accept.

Jim: When these people are cashing out, you said in many cases they do, that's when they eventually can take their own loan on the property and they take a traditional mortgage and buy out of the deal they're currently in.

Ron: Correct, unless I have it under agreement for long term and then generally I don't care if they cash me out or not. I'll give you an example. You want an example?

Jim: Yeah, I'd love an example.

Ron: Do you have time for an example?

Jim: Yeah, absolutely.

Ron: I just did a house with a $351,000 debt on it, house worth about 385. I bought it with owner financing so my purchase price is the same as theirs except that I simply make a payment on the house. Nobody got any new loans. I bought it with owner financing. I installed a lease option tenant buyer in it, Jim, who gave me a $50,000 nonrefundable option deposit and who has two years to go get a new loan. That $50,000 totally went to me. Since the seller got no money, they got exactly what they wanted which was debt relief, and I paid the closing costs, so most of that $50,000 is total net profit.

It took me two months to find that tenant buyer, put him in the house. They love it. They got two years to go clean up whatever ... I think their credit score was about 50 points too low, so they got two years to get that fixed. We even put them with a fellow who will fix that for them, and so they got two years to go get it refinanced. When I bought it from the seller, I'm not under any balloon. There's no time at which I have to pay it off. My owner financing was long-term owner financing. Seller got what they wanted. They got out. They don't have to write a check to get out. That payment is off their back. It's being made every month. Buyer got what they wanted. I got what I wanted. Everybody wins, and ultimately, the bank will get paid off and the new loan will be initiated by our new buyers.

Jim: It makes perfect sense. When you say long term with the original owner, is it like if they have 22 years left on their mortgage, are you doing a 22 year term with them?

Ron: They had 27 years left and that's the term of my loan to them, 27 years, but realistically, the loan will be paid off within the next two or three years. What difference does it make?

Jim: Right, but just it's structured ... If you're looking at it from the original owner's perspective, because that would make sense or you'd try to explain that to everybody, so you put that ... That makes a lot of sense, so $50,000 down. That has got to be unusual in a 350 property, or are you seeing that more often?

Ron: No. It's not unusual at all in a $400,000 house. I've turned down a lot of tenant buyers with less, but I knew that the property would command more. Patience allowed me to get more. You see, when you got 81% of the market who can't qualify for a loan right now, that doesn't mean they're broke and you've given them a chance to buy beautiful homes in beautiful neighborhoods, they'll come up with the money and in this particular case I just cited you, this was a double working family. They worked in the same business, but they were making pretty good money. They just had a temporary credit issue, so they got total control of the house. They got two years to get it financed. They got exactly what they wanted, and they're in this beautiful home.

This is a home behind a gate. It's only a three-year-old house, so the more dollars you wallow in, the more stick to you. In fact, I'm working with folks around the country here doing multimillion houses right now, Jim, and I don't even want to give you one of those examples. You won't sleep tonight.

Jim: Actually, I saw from this product launch you're doing for your free trainings, I actually read up on it a little bit on it; 3.9 million, is that one of the ones you're talking about?

Ron: That's one, yeah. Yeah, that's one, so those will be very nice six-figure paydays on houses we don't even own.

Jim: You just control. Same thing that basically you explained on a bigger level, is that what I'm gathering?

Ron: There's just another zero.

Jim: Yeah. Man.

Ron: But there's another zero on our paycheck, too.

Jim: That's impressive, but I guess people have banged up credit for different reasons. We know getting loans is difficult so they have to have good credit today to get a loan, especially at that size, so obviously it makes sense this is the direction you went in. Very impressive.

Ron: Not only do they have to have good credit, they have to have 20% down once you get above FHA, and we'll give them time. If they don't come to the table with 20%, then we'll take whatever they've got within reason and then give them time to pay in the other 20 before they go get a loan.

Now the house is worth 395 because the buyer and I both agreed that's what its worth, so that is what it's worth.

Jim: There's no appraisal on a lease option, so...

Ron: No, there's not, and keep in mind, two years from now, it'll be worth more than that, and they have two years to go get a loan.

Ron's Productivity Tip:

I would say let other people do what they do best and get the heck out of their way and do what you do best. What you do best is making decisions and running companies, not doing grunt work.

Jim: That's what I was gathering as I'm asking you questions and you talk about VA's and how you work three or four hours a week on this business, which obviously, doing 6 to 12 deals a month working a few hours a week is extremely impressive, so obviously, you've figured out the VA thing.

Ron: Yes.

Jim: These VA's, are they in the US? Are they outside of the US?

Ron: They're all US VA's. In fact, we have a VA system here in our building. We have a whole group of VA's that we use to serve our clients throughout the country, and our clients needed them so bad, our students needed them so bad, the only way that we could control them not getting fleeced by all kinds of companies out there was to start our own and then train them to do what needs to be done in the process of buying and selling houses, so our VA's call all the FSBO's and run them down and complete the property information sheet, do all the front end work, so before our client, our student, even gets the property information sheet, they know that the seller is predisposed to do business with them so it cuts down the amount of time they have just making a few phone calls a week and making one or two trips a week or so to get one or two contracts signed, so really, there's not much time invested in it as long as you let other people do the time-consuming tasks, and I know that's very difficult for people to understand, but if you're ever going to grow, if you're ever going to make any serious money, you got to get out of your own way and quit doing the minutia. Every time you decide you want to do minutia, you're getting paid a VA's wages.

For more information on Ron visit:

www.Ronsfreebook.com

www.RonsDollarDeal.com

Zack Childress

Zack Childress with REI Success Academy. Zack is the real deal; he's been investing in real estate for over fourteen years and currently invests in seven different markets around the US. He spent the last five years of his full-time investing career creating automated virtual investing systems, where he can invest in markets all over the country. He doesn't even have to leave his house, and I'm told he's working from his house right now during this interview to work in all seven of the markets that he's currently in.

Zack is a virtual real estate investor that uses the power of the internet to buy and sell all these properties. He's working anywhere from twenty to thirty properties at any given time. He's made investing in real estate so easy that anyone can invest in real estate; anywhere in the country you have a computer and a cell phone. He is best known as Mr. Automation and rightfully so because he continues to deliver the real estate industry automated tools and techniques that investors can use to benefit and grow their business. Zack, thank you for being here with us today, I really appreciate it.

Zack's Answer:

I always say to my students, take it all away and I would be fine because I know what I know now. Knowledge is the power, gaining the knowledge, investing in yourself, getting the tools of the trade, which is the strategies that are available to us out there is what really changes the game. It doesn't matter how many apartment units you have or how many houses you flip.

What matters is if you get it all knocked away can you rebuild again? I really think that's where the question's at, is, "Hey look, if it was all taken away, how would you rebuild again?" I always have to go back to some of fundamentals of real estate, and real estate for me ... For any successful junior investor, trying to start their real estate investing business, there's three components of capital they have to be focused on. Those three components of capital are what will allow them to build their business.

I don't mean capital like they got to have a whole bunch of money; I mean being self-sufficient is what we call an SLB, a Self Liquidating Business Model. Let me break these three down, then that'll help understand where we can start to build the business if we don't have any money. I always refer to-, capital number one is we have to have what's referred to as seed capital.

Capital meaning to get our business started to invest in our education, to really get the business off the ground and running which real estate investing is a business. Do not shy away from that, it is a business and it needs to be run that way. Where does the new investor ... Where would I get seed capital, or any new investor, right now, today in this market get capital to start their business off again? Well, I always refer to as capital one, seed capital, is referred to as Tier One Investing, and that is wholesaling.

We can go out and wholesale a piece of real estate and make a five thousand, ten thousand dollar check and that gives our new business, our brand new company that we started seed capital. We didn't have to go borrow any money or anything; we have capital right out the gate to get started. The misconception around Tier One Investing is that wholesaling is just traditional wholesaling, which is for those that don't know: you find a property at a discount, you find a cash buyer, you put a contract together with an assignment clause and you sign your rights from that contract to that cash buyer.

In return for that you get what's called an assignment fee, five or ten thousand dollars. One of the easiest and fastest ways to make money, it's how I got started, it's how I built my seed capital for my business. I didn't have money; I didn't have people to go borrow money from. As a new investor I tell them, "Stick on this plan, seed capital we got to have that is Tier One Wholesaling."

Don't get discouraged if someone says, "Yeah, but everybody's doing traditional wholesaling." Rightfully so they are, but you have to become a master wholesaler, and when you become a master wholesaler, you'll learn there's six different ways of wholesaling. One is traditional wholesaling; I'll give you a couple more. Number two is wholesaling an option, wholesaling an option means that you don't even need a cash buyer; you don't even need a buyer that has the money to go get a loan.

You just need a buyer who's willing to take over the option and pay you the option fee and you wholesale the option out. Another way of wholesaling is wholesaling to a retail buyer. A lot of people say, "Well how's that possible Zack?" Well, it's possible when you get out there and you've been doing it as long as I have and you realize you don't want to compete with everybody else who's doing traditional wholesaling.

I've perfected a form called, Wholesaling to a Retail Buyer, and what this is, is this is being able to wholesale a property that's at eighty, eighty-five, ninety percent of ARV, After Repair Value, to a buyer who's getting a loan. We've always been taught in the investing world, as junior investors, to wholesale you got to have a cash buyer. Imagine your life as a wholesaler if you didn't have to just depend on cash buyers, but you could depend on buyers who were getting financing?

As a wholesaler, you could get paid out of escrow and be put on the HUD statement as a payout fee. That, my friends, is when you're starting to build your wholesaling game. When we look at Tier One, which is what creates our seed capital to get our business off the ground, we have to look at Tier One as our wholesaling, it doesn't take money to do it, and you can go out and control properties and sell your rights to those properties.

As we move the business further, so that junior investor is getting started, they're out there they're making some money, they're building they're seed capital up, they're reinvesting in their education maybe getting a coach, or something to help build their business. Well now they have to move to income stream number two, and income stream number two is what we call, Stabilizing Income. This is the income that every business has to have to stabilize the business.

Meaning that this is the income that we can depend on, that we can count on, every single month it comes in whether or not we get out of bed, or whether or not we do any work. This stabilizing income is what we use for our marketing budget, it's what we use for hiring staff, it's what we use to get an office. It's that income that we can now build a budget and say, "Look, this is why our business can sustain itself." Don't forget we're not stopping wholesaling, so wholesaling we're still making, but this stabilizing income, three/four thousand dollars a month can help us now start to stabilize our business so that we can now focus on the growth of the business.

Tier Two Investing, or capital number two which is stabilizing capital, we refer to that as, "Where do we get it at? Where do we get this money?" We look at that as a Tier Two Investing Strategy. Our stabilizing income comes from a Tier Two Investing Strategy which is creative finance, which is controlling properties that can produce cash flow without ever buying the property. The beauty of it is, is when I was doing this really heavy in California, I controlled over thirty houses in California, never owned any of them, and I was absorbing the cash flow off of each one of these houses.

I was bringing in roughly twelve to fourteen thousand dollars a month off of properties I never owned. I had stabilized my business that I knew every month I was going to make anywhere from ten to fourteen thousand a month, which allowed me to hire more staff. Put more marketing out into the marketplace, to really start to grow the business by creating lead generation.

I try to keep people on this focus, "Let's focus on Tier One to create seed capital. Once we get that up and running and going, now let's move into Tier Two so that we can create stabilizing capital." Which is controlling properties, and there's a plethora of ways to control properties, you can control them through Lease Options, Sandwich Lease Options, Subject-to's, you can control them through seller financing, land contract, contract for deeds. There's a lot of ways to do this. The beauty of that Tier Two is it allows that new investor, that's not in a position yet to go to a bank, get a traditional loan and buy rental property, to now start building rental portfolio properties in their portfolio without buying anything. That's where the stabilizing income comes in. Now-, now we're building a business, so now we're in this. We understand we're wholesaling to create seed capital. We understand we're creating stabilizing capital through controlling properties that produce cash flow, without buying them.

Now we're at a point where most investors would be extremely happy, because if you think about it, just those two processes alone, I've not spent any of my money to get started again. I've simply worked the process. I've taken it one step at a time, to build the process to where I want to be by utilizing strategies that allow me to take advantage of the different lead sources that come in. Because if the lead comes in and the seller owes a hundred thousand, and they want ninety-five thousand, most investors would say, "That's no deal." Well, that's wrong, that's a Tier Two deal all day long.

You just got to know how to use the right strategy for the right lead, which builds the business. Now they're stabilized in their business, the next process to any business, it doesn't matter if they're selling widgets on the side of the road, or if they're doing real estate investing, they have to now grow that business. That business has to start growing; if it doesn't grow then it will eventually fade off. Where do we get growth capital at? Do we go out now to find investors who invest in our business, and give us capital, and help us grow? What if we don't want to do that? What if we don't want to be tied down with that type of liability? Or what if we don't want to give up a piece of our company to bring in an investor into our business and let them buy into shares?

Being self-liquidated means that you're doing it on your own, the third type of capital, the growth capital, comes from a Tier Three Investing. Tier Three Investing is just that, it is where we get large chunks of money based on our knowledge of the industry, so that we can now take forty, and fifty, and sixty thousand dollar chunks of capital and reinvest it in our business, and maybe move into a different market now. Maybe move into multiple markets, or maybe buy a building that we're going to move our office into, or maybe start to invest that into more wealth models so that we can have a three year retirement plan.

Tier Three investing comes from fix and flips. This is a little bit more risky than Tier One, Tier Two but rightfully so, there's bigger payouts from it, and you don't just jump into that out the gate if your building your business correctly you can go from Tier One, to Tier Two, to Tier Three so now you have the experience. You have the knowledge, you've been out there communicating with people. You've got an understanding of the basics of investing and the common mistakes that can be made and you have a knowledge base and you invested in your education.

Tier Three investing is all about fix and flips, it's about finding those diamonds in the rough, getting in there and investing capital to fix them. People say, "Well Zack, if you're going to do Tier Three don't you got to have your own money in it?" No, you don't, because think about this: If I go after Tier Three Investing I can find a private or a hard money lender very easy, all I got to do is Google it, "Hard money lender, my city and state." And I'll find them. They'll fund the purchase.

That also leaves a gap right, called Bridge Funding, which is-, there's a gap there which is what we got to have as the fix-up capital. If you think about the model I just explained, if our Tier Two is our stabilizing capital, it's what's paying our everyday expenses and maybe paying us a payroll. Our Tier One's still running, so our Tier One, our five, ten, fifteen thousand dollar wholesale bills are starting to add up now.

Now as soon as I build up an extra twenty, or thirty thousand dollars in reserves, well now I can go out into Tier Three. I can get a hard money lender to buy the house, I can come in with my twenty thousand for the fix-up and boom, I can fix it, get it on the market, sell it. I can make forty thousand off that deal, put the twenty thousand back in my pocket that I put into it.

Now I've got forty thousand dollars in a reserve for growth capital that I can choose to do whatever I want with it. Like I said, move into another market, take on a different strategy, and maybe move into some long term wealth. Maybe move into Tier Four, which is passive investing, start buying fourplexes and eight units. If you think about that one, two, three model none of that required me to use any of my money to get started and it is a process for any new or junior investor to really take serious if they want to know how to build the business successfully to where the business is basically running on its own foundation and you're not just being volatile or high risk.

You've actually jumped out there; you've laid a solid concrete foundation before you started building the first floor of walls, so that you could then build the second story. I thought long and hard about that question, and I thought, "Oh well and easy answer would be, 'Oh well let's just go wholesale and make some money.'" But I felt like if I answered it that way that would be really doing the reader or the listener a disservice because this is really a business. This isn't a get rich overnight business, this is a business and if we're going to build it that way, we need to really understand, "How can I really build this business over the next twelve months with a very solid growth pattern that I can stick to?"

Those would be the three processes I would tell anybody, anybody to go through because it's what I went through. It's the exact model I went through to build what I built. It's the exact model I teach my high level coaching students. That's how come they do so well, so we put the blinders on, we stop focusing on all the distractions and we just work on Tier One.

Then we move to Tier Two, and then we move to Tier Three and by the time they're at Tier Three, they've already got a successful business and they've spent no money out of their pocket unless they've reinvested money that they've been making off of Tier One back into their education, or back into their systems or tools, or their knowledge base, or hiring a mentor which is highly important to any business.

I have mentors myself and most successful people out there will tell you that they built their business because of having a mentor in their life as well. To keep it kind of short, and not turn this into a four hundred-page book, I would say that those three fundamentals would help any new person get out the gate and get going.

Zack's Productivity Tip:

Some of these are going to be so simple, which is really the beauty behind it: Google Drive, Skype, and my smart phone. Those three things I could not live without, to be honest with you. I know that's so simplistic it's not like this secret tool out there, but I run my entire business off of Google Drive.

From the spreadsheets, to the documents, to everything is on Google Drive. I don't just run one business off of Google Drive; I have seven companies that I run off of Google Drive. That helps me stay productive, because my calendars are on there, my Google Calendars, everything's on there. From my phone, no matter where I'm at, I can pull up a spreadsheet see where our deals are at and the flow from my deal.

My acquisitions managers, I can pull up spreadsheets to see where my accountant issues are, I can pull up spreadsheets and see where project management's going on. I can pull up docs; I can send docs, I Skype no matter where I'm at. I can do virtual phone Skyping. I'm addicted to Google by the way, because I also use a lot of what's called Google Voice. We use Google for everything when it comes to the app components of it: Google Drive, Google Voice, Google Calendar, and all that stuff.

Jim: Yeah, that's ... That is a great ... I mean I learned years ago, somebody-, a person at a very high level just like you are told me the same thing, "Use Google for-" We're talking like a business that was doing eighty million or something crazy and he's like, "We run it off Google by the way, Google Drive, Google Calendar, that's what we use. We're going to use it forever, it's free, it's great and why wouldn't we-, why would we use anything else?"

Zack: And it's real-time active; as soon as they enter information I get it, as soon as I enter information they get it. And Skype, I couldn't do without Skype too. Here's what I love about Google Drive, or Google in itself, is just how simplistic it is, but also let me just say this, I run seven companies that all do over seven figures a year by themselves, and we do it all from Google Drive, so whoever told you that was a smart man.

For more info on Zack and his company visit:

www.REISuccessAcademy.com

Mark Evans, DM

Now Mark has a massive real estate investing empire, and he does this all virtually while traveling the world. If you don't believe me, check out his Facebook page because this guy just goes all over the place. He's also a seven-time best-selling author. He's a creator of multiple innovative, cutting-edge real estate software systems; he has a popular podcast called "The Real Estate Power Hour." This is the go-to real estate investing coach for the gurus. I mean, this guy teaches the top guys how to do real estate investing and he has students all around the world. This is all from a guy whose high school teachers thought that he wouldn't even graduate high school. Mark, thanks for being here with me today.

Mark's Answer:

Yeah, that's a great question. I wish I could answer fully without going back and forth, but real quick: the virtual thing. A lot of people always give me slack for "what does virtual mean?" Knowing someone's got to look at the property, touch the property, smell the property, and all that. Virtual, to me ... You're familiar with Michael Gerber, The E-Myth, right?

So, virtual to me is about having a business. As you know, most people in the industry, and businesses period, they don't have a business. They have a glorified job. They work for a maniac, maniac being you, as us the individual ... So virtual to me ... Yes, I live in Palm Beach, Florida, my properties are mostly in the Midwest, pretty much all of them, and I haven't been to a property since 2006, but we have systems and people in place, and processes. We have a virtual business. I have a COO, we have sales guys that are in the office here in Palm Beach. We have on-the-ground teams and all that. So when people think virtual often times I think they get an idea as if nothing happens. It's just kind of like, "Oh it's all fake, it's in the air, and I'm hanging out on the beach, getting money back and forth virtually." There's really a lot of work that goes into this, but setting it up ... Virtual, really, I guess what I'm saying is a mindset and a business process, as opposed to just fluff in the air.

Yeah, so your first question is: if I didn't have a lot of money ... So, I think that that's the first question I'd like to address, because what does that mean? It's all relative. Bill Gates, a lot of money to him might be different to me or you.

What does a lot of money mean when you say to that?

Jim: Well, it's limited, like you have a small budget. You can't spend five grand a month on marketing. You might have a budget, let's just say you could spare five hundred a month for marketing, at the beginning of your real estate ... 'Cause you don't really know what to do when you still have a job and you have other...

Mark: Well, I think the number one thing is ... Unfortunately, I see this every day, and I'm sure people see this and may even be a part of it. Everyone's going out and buying seminars and twenty-dollar books and all this stuff, which is great to start with, but they're doing it ... and I call them "seven-year newbie syndrome." They've been "studying" for seven years, and you're saying five hundred dollars is a budget. I would bet a lot of the big-name people don't even spend five hundred a month 'cause they don't know how to. Most people are focused on techniques and tactics, as opposed to business growth, development, on marketing, and such. Which, as you know, you and I both spend money on marketing 'cause we understand the importance of it.

So, to me ... I think if you're starting out, you could do it for ... Depending on what you're good at ... I always say start with your ideal lifestyle and start with what your gifts are. Because either you have resources or your resourcefulness. If you're sitting at home, watching Maury Povich and eating Doritos and drinking beer, you probably don't have the same skillset as I or you Jim.

So you might need to invest a lot of money in your marketing to get going, 'cause no one knows who the hell you are 'cause you're not out there doing anything. You're sitting in your house, hiding, hoping and praying and dreaming that things are going to happen, and that's just not how this business works. And, then you have the other side of the person ... the person that's hustling, the person that's out there driving for dollars every day ... driving around the town, knowing their market, being smart about it. And that's another thing I see that makes me sick, is ... And again, where I'm getting to the answer here, Jim, is I drive around for seven days in Columbus, Ohio, where I'm from ... When I was eighteen years old I could tell you exactly what street, what zip code, what houses, what they look like, what they're near ... I knew the market 'cause I invested the time in it. What I see every single day is so many people are just so busy learning that they're not doing.

So if I was going to say what marketing ... You don't have to spend a dime on marketing to do a deal or two deals. What you have to do is you have to actually get up and do something. You have to call twenty buyers a day, call twenty sellers a day. Talk to them. See what's going on. How can you benefit them? Don't call them and say "Hey, how can you benefit me?" Become valuable to them. And that's really a guerrilla marketing approach. I started with ... When you say "very little" ... I started with negative money.

I was dead broke. I was eighteen years old, had no money, had no credit, just got out of high school, never went to college, scared as hell ... But I wasn't scared of what I didn't know, I was more afraid of what I did know. So I had to change my situation. The only way is something different, to get different results. So, if you're looking just to do a couple deals to get going, to get some money in the bank, go on Craig's List, drive for dollars. I mean ... Jim, as you know, the We Buy House signs are everywhere. Go on Craig's List, type in the We Buy Houses and all these different locations, and people want to do deals. Guys like you and I, Jim, we buys deals. If we buy deals, that means we're making money.

So, people call me and say ... well, they don't call me, but they'll call my sales staff and say: "Mark, I have this awesome deal. It's thirty-two thousand, it's ... "Just give me the basic numbers. I know my market, so if 32k makes sense, we're buying it. You don't need to sell me, you don't need to be a slick salesman or anything, you just need to be valuable as a person ... bringing me a deal that I might not know is available. That'd be an easy way to pop off two to five grand wholesale fees.

I love direct mail, Jim. It's the most predictable, profitable thing I've ever done. We've invested tens of millions of dollars over the years to direct mail. We still do direct mail every single day today. I love the internet for that, as well. When I say "direct mail" I'm talking online, solo email broadcasting, as well as direct mail to motivated sellers and marketplaces that we're looking to work in. It's really just being consistent and understand that. But there is another side to that.

Often times, say if you spend five hundred dollars ... There's an old adage we have that we say: "We just don't know what we don't know." One of the guys came into my group that we do, and he's like "Mark, I've been doing direct mail instead of ... " I think he was spending eight hundred bucks a month, but getting very small results ... like a two percent response which he feels is good. And how he's handling the lead is a big key.

You know, what happens is a lot times people are doing intake marketing, so they'll send out a postcard, they'll put their cell phone number on it, they're hanging out at Rooster's having some beers and wings, they'll get a phone call. There's no formalities, there's not process, there's no procedure. Again, it's job. It's not a business. What we do is we actually paint a picture. If you send a thousand post cards in, you get 200 calls back in the next 3 days and you're taking those inbound. How in the world would you handle that? We send them through a 2 or 3 minutes process recording line. They listen, we tell them exactly who we are, what we do, how we do it. Again, how I feel like we win is we call them at a specific time. Everyday, our sales teams walk in, they have leads, they know what to do and their job is, this is a huge take away for everyone, listen in a reading, consult the selling.

You know, we're 2000 almost 15 now. People are out there just selling to sell. What we do is we actually listen, we want to guide them. If we have a better solution that we know exists, we tell them about it. Often times, they won't even take the better solution for them, they just want a solution. What we do is, again, consult the selling key. Again, I think people's marketing ... I don't think, I know for sure, marketing dollars can go so much further if you just start looking at your process, your procedure and start looking, "How can I make this better?" Often times, what's funny, Jim, and

I see this every day. People just throw more money at it. They're like, "Well I need more leads, I want us to more money into it." Often times, the majority, 98% of the time probably. It's not about spending more money to get more leads, it's about taking what you have and making better. Getting more defined, getting more streamlined, getting more focused, and getting more focused on the clients. Maybe your call back times are different, maybe the prospect framing's different but just getting more focused on your process and procedures.

We'll call them back … Oh no, we call them back and … So we don't just call them back. We'll call them, we'll email them, we'll text them. There's a million different ways to get to people today. Again, this is if you're lazy, you just call them back 3 times and you hang up. Well there's not … No, people are busy. They don't time for you. They don't time for us, they don't have time for anybody. That's why they're motivated, they're trying to sell. You got to picture … the problem is, again, it's not about us. If we said, "Hey, we only called them 3 times, that's it." It's about a sales process, it's about a process. I mean, we have guys we've called 17 times or more. Through emails, through voice broadcast or whatever. Then we get them on the phone, these are busy professionals sometimes. Busy investors, they have a lot going on. They found out add, they got our postcard or whatever. We call them. Again, what's it take? 13 seconds to make a dial? It's easy. So we put them on the file, we follow up with them 3 days from now. Boom, 3 days from now, boom. Within 3 months, they're going to get hit from us a lot and we keep them in our system forever.

Buy or die or tell us, "Hey, we're just not interested." You got to also understand too, Jim, is when you're consultive selling right? You're listening. Everyone … Again, we deal with a lot of investor sellers. The way our marketing goes through direct mail process, I know you do this as well, but we mail. We direct mail a lot of people that are not owner occupied properties. If you just think for second, I wrote my first course back in 2004 called "Reverse Real Estate". All I did was reverse engineer the process. That process was go get buyers and then get deals. Same time with this. When we reverse engineer this and we're going after non-owner occupied folks, we realize that they don't like in the house. They either inherited it or they're investors that bought it and they rent it out. When these people call us back and then we call them back we asked them what's going on. They might say, "Hey, I'm not looking to sell." Great, are you looking to buy? Just a simple question. Instead of saying, "Okay, thanks, goodbye." Then you look in the mirror, you say, "I'm a loser, this doesn't work. I bought all these courses, I knew this didn't work. It was too good to be true." Instead, it's not a matter of what we're doing it's a matter of what we're not doing. We ask that one question, you'll kick up your buys list by 12 to 15%. Just the one question. Then you don't have to spend anymore money on marketing.

Again, as your business grows. You might be thinking, 'Oh, 10, 15%. That's not much." We get thousands and thousands and thousands of leads a week, 10 or 15% is a massive change. We live in a society where people are lazy as hell and it drives me crazy. Not a lot of work, it's kind of a relative term too because to me it's pretty easy. Right? As a opposed to waking up, jumping in the car at 8 o'clock, driving an hour to work, hating my boss, hating the people I work with, getting a 15 minute break and then a half hour lunch break, and then trying beg my boss … I'm a 55-year-old guy let's say, begging my boss to take off to go see my kids recital. To me that's bullshit. You're 55-years-old, grow a pair of balls and step up to plate and let's get serious about life. Really, what it comes down to, if we're being 100% honest, is people don't know what the hell they want. They want to talk the game but don't want to do the game. It's not hard. It's very easy to get on the phone and call 20 sellers and 20 buyers. We all could do that today. I don't care who you are, where you live, what your financial situation is or anything.

Right. Craigslist is all free. So if you are in the beginning stages, that's a great way. Just get dirty making calls. It's funny, Jim, a guy you and I know, Mark, he's actually in your market. He's not sitting at home, because you said,"Yeah, he shared a property with me. It was too high." Mark's not sitting at home crying about, "Oh, well Jim's not buying my property." What he's doing is figuring out who will buy it and going after them and talking to them and creating communications and staying in front of you. If you don't buy this property, you don't write them off. He doesn't say, "Jim's not serious buyer." What's her doing to do next week or next day? He's going to market to you another property.

It just comes down to he's just doing it. This is what most people don't do. They'll go spend $30,000 or $50,000 for a mentor. The best mentor you'll ever do is go buy an investment property. You'll learn more about what a HUD is, instead of reading about it or thinking you know what it is. What a title company does, what their job and role is. What a property management company does.

What all these things do. If you pay $50,000 cash for a house which you can easily do on my market, 30 to 50, at least the worst case scenario, you have something to show for it. I would almost guarantee anybody that goes out and does that model, just goes out and ... I'm not saying mentoring is not important, because I actually had mentors and everyone I know does. There is a time and place when enough of the mentoring and learning. Stop learning and start doing. When you do that, that will be your biggest mentor.

Yeah, that'd be a mid-west property. Like Ohio, Georgia, you can buy stuff in there. These are probably areas we won't want to live in but they're decent. You could walk there at night and not get shot. I'm not saying it's deep in the hood.

Not war zones, but you're going generate 15 to 20% net ROI on your money if you run the deal right.

Here's the thing, it's again, Jim. I always say it ... I see people that will spend $25,000 on mentoring ... Let's say $30,000 because it's a property. So they'll spend $30,000 on mentoring, they'll wake up 3 years from now and they don't have anything to show for it except $30,000 in dept. If you buy a $30,000 house, you could sell it for $15,000 pretty easy right? At least you get half your money back and you actually did a deal.

At least you've done something. Again, it's just getting over ... "What do I charge? How much do I charge for this? What strategy ..." Sit down and say, "What is my gift? Am I good at sells? Am I good at this? Am I good at marketing? Am I good at talking to people? Am I good at financing?" You got to find out where you're good at and just get really strong with it and find people that are bad at it. That's why co-whole selling is powerful is because … Jim, you're great, you love buying, fixing, and selling. Mark hates it, the guy in your market. He does a couple of them but he hates it. That's not how he's geared. He hands it off, you make money he makes money. Everyone's happy. Could he make more? Yes. Could he make less? Yes. But that's what investing is.

Again, that's how you have that skill set. You have that mental threshold, that business understanding threshold. I'm not saying Mark doesn't because I think he's very smart on that side but that's not what he enjoys. He doesn't like dealing with that piece even if it's just one little piece because that's not his personality. He'd rather sit in his house, do what he does, send an email whatever and make money and he does pretty well financially. He does real well.

Yeah, the only thing different though, you're doing retailing. It's all the same game, the biggest thing that we're really saying … The really silver lining here is you and I aren't afraid to mess up. We know that we're not going to be right 100% of the time, but our winners are going to overcome our losers. Most people are sitting on the sideline trying figure out how to make more, how do I not get ripped off, how do I do this or how do I do that? Then they how do themselves to death. Then they wake up 7 years later, they've spent a $100,000 on mentoring, they've never done a deal because they're afraid to mess up and they still don't know what to do. Now they've listened to 20 different strategies, they know all these things that exist. Being green is probably the best thing you could do. Only know 1 or 2 strategies. Just go do it and become the best at it and you'll make millions.

Jim:	Yeah, I couldn't agree more. Just focus on one thing. Don't be, what do they say? The jack of all trades, master of nothing?
Mark:	Yeah. At the end of the day, real estate all the same core concepts. You have to have a buyer, you have to have a seller. Right? Pretty simple. Everything else is just details. Is it your money? I don't know. If you have a lot of money, maybe it is your money. If you have a lot time, maybe you have more time than money. All these things are fine. They key is stop making excuses, pull up your panties, and get serious about life. I mean that's really ... That's honestly,

Jim, that's what I think I told you. We work with high level people that are doing deals because I don't like people that make excuses.

People that are successful, we say, "Yes, we can that. No. Yes okay good I'm in." We're very quick and decisive. Indecision is no decision.

That's exactly how the business works though, right? Because that's kind of what happens. Some gets aggressive, they go watch a TV infomercial, they go to a seminar, they do that, they buy a property and then they're like, "Oh my god, this actually takes work." And then they say, "I don't want to deal with that, I'm busy. I have 3 kids, I have school, I have church, I have all this stuff." Again, they just aren't ... If you want to quit your job, this is the only way I know how to do it in this business. Just get started. You can make literally time for dollars, thousands of dollars an hour. Thousands.

Jim: A follow up question I have in this and it's productivity habit or tool that you use on a daily basis. You've kind of answered that in how you built your business. Maybe you'd share something, but that's a follow up question I've been asking everybody. If you had one productivity habit or toll you use on daily basis to produce results you do, what would that be? I mean, I've heard several examples of that in your response already. But if you want to answer that...

Mark's Productivity Tip:

That's a great question. I'd love to answer it. I think it's really two things. One, wake up to do it. Get out there and do it, don't be afraid to mess up. And two, pick up the damn phone. It is your friend. Call people and genuinely want to help them. They don't care if you're about to go bankrupt, they don't care if your kids like you, they don't care if hate your job, they don't care about you at all. It's just the life to business. So when I pick up the phone and I call people, it's not about me, it's not about what we can make or can't make. It's about how can we best serve them or how can we help them? So pick up the phone. You just got call and want to help people.

Well, there are two reasons people don't answer their phones. One, you're ignorant and after you read this, you can't do that ever again. And/or two, you just don't care about your life or your financial future or you family. Look at you mom, your dad, your kids, your spouse, the people you care most about, look at them and just say, "I really just don't care. I'm going to be lazy. I'm going to be ignorant. I'm not going to take this serious. I'm just going to play around with it and mickey mouse around and complain how it doesn't work." That's the only reason that that doesn't work. You have to get serious with this stuff. This is real life business. This is life and it can change your life and everyone you care about's life.

As you know Jim, I was just out in the Caribbean on a boat for the last 7 days with very, very, ultra limited email. Dial up was quicker. Zero cellphone ... What's that? It was awesome, it was one of my dreams I wanted to do and again, I looked at my wife and I said, "We're living too small.' There are certain things that we are scared of, even of our own success. I can afford a yacht, it's not going to change my life either way, but I was holding off on it but truthfully, at the end of the day, you got to find people around you that will pick you up and push you forward. Start up-leveling your life on many levels. It's something I've been wanting to do since I was 7-years-old, I was going to do it in 2016. I decided to do it on a whim with one of buddies. One of my mentors actually. Just to reiterate that, I did not make one phone call. Zero phone calls for 8 days, we closed 14 deals. I didn't make one email to my assistants because things are being handled. Everything's handled. That's the purpose of setting up a business. And there's a lot power to that.

For more information on Mark and his company visit:

www.MarkEvansDM.com

Or on Facebook at Mark Evans DM

Larry Goins

Larry Goins, is the author of the bestselling book *"Getting Started in Real Estate Day Trading"*. It's in book stores everywhere as well as his latest book, *"HUD Homes Half Off"*, which we're going to give you an opportunity to get for free today, this book teaches you how to buy HUD homes at 50%, 40% even 30% of the list price, which is incredible!

Over the last 10 years, Larry's traveled the country and the world speaking at large real estate Investor clubs, conventions, expos. He's been on stage with guys like Tony Robbins, Robert Kiyosaki and Donald Trump just to name a few. These are the legends of real estate investing and this guy's on stage with them. If you are investing in real estate today, if you're new to real estate investing or you've been in real estate investing for a while, Larry can teach you how to take your business to the next level.

Larry's Answer:

Well I think it would depend on a couple of things. It would depend on number one, do I have

any money to get started? And number two; if I don't have any money to get started, what's the fastest, easiest way to find what's called unadvertised properties? Reason being, you can assign the contracts for unadvertised properties. Maybe I'm using some terms that people don't understand throughout this interview, but it's okay; it's all explained in my book that they're going to get for free. When you're working with unadvertised properties, like for example, you put out some bandit signs, you know those signs that say "We buy houses," or "I buy houses", have your phone number on them. We actually pay people $1 per sign to put them out and we have people all over the states of North and South Carolina putting those out and we get on average I'm guessing about 25 to 30 calls a day from those signs.

Now not all of the deals work out, but the good news is, when you find a deal using that strategy you can absolutely get it under contract and use the term "and/or assigns". This means you could put up a $10 or $100 deposit and then just assign that contract. That's if you have no money to put in the deal yourself. Now, if you have a little bit of money to put up for a deposit, say $500, I can show you how to buy HUD houses as well. HUD houses are by far my number one source of properties. I'm the largest buyer in North Carolina, according to HUD's own attorney. About 65% to 70% of the 10 to 20 deals a month that we do are HUD properties and we're now expanding into other states. In fact, we've just launched 5 additional states. I'm based in Lake Wylie, South Carolina, but I do deals all over both the Carolinas. I've just launched Virginia, Tennessee, Georgia, Alabama, and Kentucky, and we're going to be buying HUD houses in those states as well.

Jim: Was there something specific about those states that makes HUD properties attractive or just because they're kind of close to where you're at?

Larry: Well yeah, they're all around me. It doesn't really make sense to go from the Carolinas to upstate New York, Ohio, Pennsylvania, or Arizona or somewhere; so we're just expanding out here. Now instead of being the largest buyer of HUD houses in the Carolinas, my goal is to be the largest buyer in the Southeast. That's just one of our goals. Our plan is to do 260 deals in next year, this coming year I should say, which we're almost there. That's going to be averaging around 5 closings a week. We're already doing 3 to 5. Sometimes we'll have 0 or 1 or 2, but then sometimes we'll have more than 5. They're not all HUD properties. About 60-70% of our deals are HUD deals and the neat thing about HUD houses is the fact that it's all done on computer. We actually have virtual assistants in the Philippines that we hire, and I show you how to do that in my book, but we have VA's that we hire to go out and analyze these deals. They spend about 6 to 10 minutes per house analyzing. They put it on this special spreadsheet that I've created, which by the way is in the book for free, and we merge it with HUD's spreadsheet.

Then my virtual assistant, that I pay $3 an hour located in the Philippines, sits there and analyzes the deal by pulling comps on websites like zillow.com, trulia.com, cyberhomes.com, eppraisal.com. They pull rent comps, they drive the street on Google Earth, they look at all the pictures and they put 2 numbers on the spreadsheet. They put the after repaired value and the amount of repairs needed. When we do that, the spreadsheet automatically calculates how much we should offer on the property and that's it…all done by computer. Then I have another VA that sits in front of the computer every day all day long doing nothing but entering HUD bids at hudhomestore.com. Is that cool or what?

That's what we do and then we have a girl that's very good on the phone. She takes all of our sign calls, our direct mail calls, anything from ads, CraigsList, whatever it is. She is the one that takes all those calls and she's very non-threatening, very laid back, very passive, but she's able to get information that she needs to be able to pass along to our acquisition guys so we can get a property under contract. We got a deal under contract just yesterday from a bandit sign that a person had put out for us, and the owner called in and this property has an after-repaired value of around 120k and needs about 20k in repairs and we were able to get the property for, I think it was $33,000; so do the math. That's not a bad deal right there.

Jim :No, that's a pretty good deal. This is awesome information Larry. Let me ask you, as somebody that produces at the level you do, you've got to have some productivity habits, tricks or tools you use on a daily basis to produce the results that you have. Do you have one that you could share with us? Something you do every day that helps you keep focused, even if it's just a tool, a gadget, technology wise or something else?

Larry's Productivity Tip:

Well, I think that everybody's always really into these apps and different software's and automated things and done for you and all this. We use software, we use a few CRMs, one's called Podio another is Infusionsoft. You can go out there and you can get email programs like Constant Contact, iContact, you can use all these latest software programs, but I've got to tell you if I was brand new and just getting started, man I would just order 100 bandit signs, I would go put them out at busy intersections, I would get a Google Voice number, keep a check on the phone and then I would go out, meet with the people and negotiate a deal.

You can get Larry's free book at:

www.FreeHUDbook.com

Mike Hambright

Mike Hambright is the host of the #1 podcast on real estate investing, FlipNerd. Now, Mike's been a real estate investor for years. He's bought and sold hundreds of properties himself and in the last few years he's been a mentor to teams of investors all over the country that buy collectively around a thousand houses a year. That's a ton of properties this guy is helping guys flip and do and teach on, so if you've seen his podcast, you know what I'm talking about. If you haven't, I highly recommend you go check it out. But he dedicates much of his time now to teaching others in the real estate investing world how to achieve financial freedom.

Mike's Answer:

That's a good question. The tricky part is without much money. I believe that it's a much easier business if you have money because this is a lead generation type business. But there are some things that if you have the hustle in you that really it's a way to get a lot of leads that a lot of people aren't willing to work hard enough for so today I'm going to talk about really the importance of networking and I'll kind of break it down into two different categories of networking so that is really kind of networking with other investors, people that you could potentially sell houses to or you could buy houses from, and I'll come back to that.

First I'll talk about networking with what I'll call referral business, people that could bring leads to you. It could be different types of attorneys, bankruptcy attorneys, probate attorneys, code compliance officers, mailmen, people that focus on elderly care. Just people that may come across deals that are not necessarily real estate investors themselves, in fact probably not. That's where the magic comes in is they're kind of off the radar and not a lot of people know about them. The question is whether you're willing to work hard enough to build these relationships.

The reason that most don't spend a lot of time in this area is it's very unpredictable. You're going to spend time building relationships with people that you're never going to get a house from, you're never going any benefit in terms of your business out of. But if you cast a wide enough net and you build enough of these relationships, then deals will come around. It's a hard business to scale, it's kind of a hard channel to scale if you will, but there's virtually no competition there and so it's kind of like direct mail in the regard that the key really is to do a lot of it and to do it consistently.

I want to give a few tips for people that are doing this. Everybody can imagine, "Hey, I'm going to go out and I'm going to meet some people, I'm going to meet some ..." let's just say bankruptcy attorneys. Now, this is what most people, if they think they're good at networking I ask this question all the time. I say, "Hey, if you think you're good at networking, you go to real estate investor events or networking events and you meet people, raise your hand." If I'm talking to a group of people that are typical real estate investors or new real estate investors, pretty much everybody will raise their hand. I'll say, "Now keep your hand up until this doesn't define you."

I say, "You fill your pockets with business cards." Everybody's hand stays up. "Come home from events." Everybody's hand stays up. "Wrap rubber band around block of cards that you've just collected." Everybody's hand stays up. "Then you'll throw it in a drawer to never be seen again." It's like, gosh, you spend all this time networking or meeting people and then we tend to just, a lot of people define networking as "Well, I met somebody." It's like, yeah, but the type of people that I'm talking about, you're not going to meet them today and they have a deal for you tomorrow. They're going to have a deal maybe never, but maybe in 6 months or in 2 years or whatever.

Really where the magic comes in is to continue to build that relationship and maintain those relationships over time so that you're top of mind if and when they ever come across a deal, then you're the first person they think of. In fact, you might be the only person that they think of because they're off the radar in terms of a lead source. I'd say, without getting into a lot of detail because I know we have limited time, there's a way to continue to build those relationships whether you're using a spreadsheet or a simple CRM program.

Just to check in with everybody once a month, once a quarter. Heck, you could even use an auto-responder that maybe you're sending a message out to 300 people and it's the same message, just saying, "I just came across a really nasty house, the ones I told you that we buy. Here's a picture of it by the way, and I just want you to remember if you ever happen to come across anything, I'm your guy." Something as simple as that and you just position yourself to be top of mind.

I'll give you an example of one for myself. This was a while back. I happen to have my company's brand on my shirt and I went to an HOA meeting where I live. There was a woman there and she said, "You're a real estate investor?" I was like, "Yeah." "Well, my grandma. Her sister's grandmother passed away 4 years ago and they've just been sitting on this house. Nobody's done anything and they need to get rid of it." She was kind of the liaison between her sister who has some health issues as well and sure enough within a week or so I looked at the house, got another contract and then, here's the magic to that.

Shame on me, that was a lead I'll be honest, where I didn't continue to build that relationship over time but miraculously, we treated her right and everything and then the sister that we bought the house from actually passed away, so the original contact called me 2 years later and said, "Well, we need to sell our sister's house now," and I was the guy. I literally bought 2 houses from this contact all because I had a branded shirt on and I was at a networking type event, which happened to be an HOA meeting of all places that had nothing to do with my business. It was my personal house.

I used that example because it's really in some ways a poor way to continue the networking relationship but if you continue to build those relationships with people over time, and maybe share some of your experiences on houses every once in awhile, like, "Here's one we bought. Here's the before and after pictures," people love to see that stuff and you're just positioning yourself as top of mind if they come across a lead.

Jim: The part about staying in touch with them, because you're right, most people at these networking events, and I'm guilty, I went through I had my hand up the whole time you said that and put the thing in the drawer. Everybody listening has done that because it's exactly what happens.

Mike: Yeah, you get busy and you think that the magic is in actually meeting people but it's just like in a relationship with your spouse. You date for awhile and over time that's where the magic starts to happen. I guess there's such thing as a one-night stand but we won't get into that here. My point is usually, just to use a cheesy cliché from where we just left, you're not going to get a lot of action unless you take some time to build these relationships.

Then I want to talk a little bit about networking with real estate investors. It's some of the same things I just said. When you build these relationships, work them over time. Build those relationships up. One of the problems is I think a lot of folks in real estate investing, and this happens to me, I'm sure it happens to you Jim. People say, "Hey, can I take you to lunch? Can I buy you lunch?" Basically, can I buy an hour of your time for 10 bucks or something like that.

I love to help people. I devote a lot of my life to it but my time is worth more than 10 bucks and just the approach of "Can I take something from you?" is a difficult one for a lot of us to swallow. I'd say try to give back whenever you can. Try to find ways to provide to people and I'll give you what I think is a good example of how you can do more deals over time. It is what I'm going to call building your own platform but using your houses, so this kind of tip assumes that you're doing some deals right now, you're doing at least one deal.

There are a lot of people that want to do what we do, buy and sell houses, whether they want to wholesale them or rehab them, whatever they might want to do. What I say is when you get a house, even if it's just one, use that as a platform for meeting more people. Let me give you a couple of examples.

For years I did a little mini-seminar if you will at houses that I was rehabbing, I'm predominately a rehabber, and I've rehabbed hundreds of houses. What I would do, I coined the term, Rehab Live. I'd have these events; I'd invite people from my local REIA club or people that are on my investor list. Anybody that was on my list I would invite to these Rehab Live events and I would actually have a 3-part meeting, so they'd come to the house 3 times or I'd invite them to come 3 times at least. Once right after we closed before we even touched it. Specifically I would use our most disgusting houses where I know there's going to be the most significant transformation.

I would invite everybody to come watch me rehab this house live. Everybody loves Flip This House and all this stuff that's on HGTV and people love the idea of experiencing that first-hand, live. Basically I would have an event 3 times. They would come at the beginning before we've done anything. Sometimes I would specifically say, "Look, do not wear flip-flops or any sort of open-toed shoes, this is gross." Then come back halfway through and then come back at the end and all along the while they'd have questions. "How did you do that?" "Why did you do that?" "What are you going to do there?" "Who's your contractor you used for that?"

I would just be a giver during that time. I'd tell them everything I know and you start to position yourself as an expert. Sure enough what happens during that kind of dance if you will, is that you find lenders, you find people that want to buy from you, you find people that come across a deal themselves and then they get afraid to rehab it or they don't want to rehab it because they just primarily want to wholesale, they'll bring you a deal because you added some value to their life by teaching them something or helping them experience something and good things happen if you do that.

You could do the same thing with a wholesale deal even if you're not rehabbing. I actually know a guy that used to have cookouts at these disgusting houses he was wholesaling, so literally have a lunchtime cookout, basically a party at a house that he's going to wholesale. He would haul a grill over there and cook hamburgers and hot dogs at lunch and he had a cooler of drinks and he didn't do that to sell the house. Especially in this market, it's not hard to sell houses if you've got them priced right, really in any market if they're priced right.

He did it as a way to build his brand, build his following of people, his network. People eat that stuff up. People want and crave experiences so if you can use the houses you have to give them experiences then that will come back around to you down the road whether it's helping you find deals, helping you find money, maybe even people that will be cash buyers for a deal that you want to wholesale to them.

I think the key in everything I just talked about here is that none of this stuff is easy. You've got to get out from behind your comfy desk or your flagship seat at the coffee shop or whatever it is, and grind it out, but this is what really separates those who are successful from those who are not. I think the stuff I talked about here is the stuff that probably a lot of people can relate to, yet probably most would agree that very few are taking the effort in working as hard as they could to differentiate themselves from all of the other people that are handing out business cards to be dropped in the drawer never to be seen again.

Jim: Think of the next step, really because you're right. Plenty of people go network in that they think it just means meeting people one time, taking their card and then we're done. But really the rapport building process and relationship building process behind that is where deals happen, right? It's rare you're going to meet somebody one time and they're going to, "Hey, I got a deal for you." It does happen. It's happened to me, I'm sure it's happened to you, but that's pretty rare.

Mike: Yeah. We're in an opportunity type business and by definition, opportunities aren't there every day. They come and go and they're few and far between relatively speaking. All the things that I just talked about here, I think it's important to position yourself as being top of mind when those opportunities come around, that people think of you and they think, "Wow, I think Jim would be interested in this because I know he buys these types of houses."

Jim: Right. Networking with investors, networking for sellers, seller leads, now the marketing portion of that, is that you're getting their contact information, emailing to them? Is there something else you do for sellers other than investors or, what marketing strategy would you focus on at the beginning? I guess networking really is one.

Mike: Yeah, I think if you're brand new and you don't have an investor list or you have no network at all, I think it has to start with going to REIA clubs and going to different events and meeting people and building up that database. Even going to, and I talked about some kind of open house or showing type events for wholesale deals, even going to some of those events, even if you have no intention on buying, just for the point of having an experience, looking at a house, getting a chance to validate whether you think their numbers are accurate or whether you think they're crazy and maybe having a chance to meet some other investors that are there because those types of events tend to draw other investors and so I think it's really just a matter of starting out someplace till you get that list built up.

Now, one of the benefits that I had was that one of the REIA clubs that I am involved with here would actually, even though it was a large group, they actually would let us post messages to the group. They had a list sort of thing where I could send an email and they had to approve it but they did and it would get blasted out to the rest of the group. But you could use, there's a lot of Facebook groups out there, there's a lot of different ways that you can get access to people that you've yet to meet and yet to build a relationship with today.

Jim: Just to touch on something you said about meeting other investors and going to meet other investors. A lot of my students initially will say, "Why am I going to meet other investors? Aren't they my competition?" Well, first of all, there are enough deals for all of us. Second of all, competition or not, whatever, I've bought so many investor overflow deals over the years from other investors, that could only do 1 or 2 deals at a time and not that there's anything wrong with doing 1 or 2 but most guys have their limit of private money, they can maybe do 5 deals at a time so if they get a 6th deal from their marketing and they can't do it, well now that can be a wholesale deal. You buy it, pay them 5 grand for the deal or whatever and you have yourself a great deal.

I've bought tons of overflow deals from investors I've networked with over the years, so that's another reason to meet other investors, and you share ideas and things that are going on in your market. Most guys are pretty open and so either way, I've bought a lot of investor overflow from other investors I met at REIA events. That's another reason to network with other investors in your market.

Mike: Yeah, absolutely. I do think one kind of a point on that is I've been in this business for a little over 6 years, not a really long time. We've had a great run, it's been a great business for us. I'd say early on I really felt more of what you talked about in terms of feeling like everybody is my competitor and I think that that's pretty typical of the individual market. It's a feast or famine business and everybody's really worried about the famine all the time so it tends to be that way.

But I think what you see is once you've been in this business for awhile, is that a lot of the people who you thought were your competitors are ... there's more opportunity if you can find ways to work together or to at least acknowledge that each other exist. There's people today that in the past I wouldn't talk to at all because I thought they were my competitor and they would say, "Hey, let's get together and have coffee and talk about stuff," and I was like, "Well, I'm rearranging my sock drawer that day. I don't have time for that." In the back of my mind I'm like, "Why would I want to talk to this guy?" But now we do deals together. They're better at some functions of what has to happen in the business.

I think the other thing is this can be a really lonely business if you let it and I think it just makes everything better if you find some friends and people that you can work with in the business because I think it depends on whether you have a scarcity mentality or you believe that there's a lot of abundance out there. Life is so much more fun if you don't have a scarcity mentality.

Jim: I couldn't agree more. I had the mindset, that's why I know. Since I've changed that and started teaching on it and going to REIAs and just sharing information, I wasn't even selling anything when I was going to these things. You were trying to meet wholesalers is what I was really doing, so I was teaching about my rehab business and hoping to meet some people that could bring me deals. That's why I was doing it and it changed my whole world. It changed everything in my business. It was the best thing I ever did. Once I just opened up and said, "Hey, screw it, let's just open up the books and show everybody what I do and how I do it."

Because I'm primarily a rehabber, too, so I was looking to meet wholesalers and it opened up so many opportunities, opportunities I never expected. It was just awesome and it was a mind shift. It took a little bit of time. It was not easy for me to come, because I was just like you, I was like, "Oh, I'm not going to meet this dude. He's my competition. I don't want to sit down with this guy." Best thing, as soon as I changed, and it was kind of by mistake that I realized it, I have to admit, but once I did it was really, it changed my whole business. My business just got better and better from there.

Mike's Productivity Tip:

Actually I'm going to piggy back on what we were talking about with networking and say that it sounds overwhelming, something we talked about, go out and meets, because you have to cast a wide net. You got to meet hundreds of people. It's kind of like direct mail, you got to send out a large amount of letters and get a very small response rate but it's kind of a numbers game. It's the same thing with a lot of stuff in this business, including networking. I would say to set small goals and know that it's okay to say, "Hey, I'm going to go meet one person every day that I could potentially buy a house from or sell a house to," and you could, you have to find the venues but it sounds easy. "Hey, could you go meet somebody today?" "Yeah, no problem. One person, yeah, sure."

By the end of the year, you got over 300 new contacts that you're grooming a relationship as we talked about and if you take it seriously, I think just knowing that it's okay to take small bites and have small goals to where every single day you're doing a little bit of something and over time it just adds up significantly. The reality is a lot of people that are in this business are one-man bands or one-woman bands or small groups of people, so it's hard to go out and do anything in huge scale unless you can afford to have a team and stuff like that. I think you're just not going to have the capacity to do anything beyond small goals, but I think I would just tell people just know that that's okay and stop fooling around and get started.

For more information on Mike and his company and/or podcast visit:

www.FlipNerd.com

Matt Andrews

Matt Andrews, CEO of The Insider Real Estate Insiders. This guy's flipped over a thousand properties all while traveling the world with his beautiful wife. He has three number one best-selling books on real estate investing on Amazon, and has a number one rated podcast called Real Estate Freedom.

On top of all of that, if that's not cool enough, this guy's working with guys like William Shatner, which is super cool especially if you're a Star Trek fan, but also, he's working with the original shark from Shark Tank, Kevin Harrington, on a product called Internet Real Estate Tycoon, and that is just super cool to me. This guy has done over three billion in product sales or something crazy like that, but anyway, hey Matt, thanks for being here with us today.

Matt's Answer:

Yeah, that's a great question. If I had to start it all over today, let's just say I was starting from zero and you dropped me off in a market that I had never been in before and just said, "Matt, start making money in real estate," what would I do? That's a great way to approach it whenever I do move into a new market because I replicate this process that I'll break down that I go through.

The first thing I would do ... No matter what my end strategy's going to be, the first thing I would do is I would find the top investor that I could find in that market. That would be step one for me. I would find whoever the number one wholesaler is or the number one rehabber or just the individual or the company that is doing the most real estate investment deals. The reason I would do that obviously is to see what the most successful person is doing, see what they're focusing on. That would be my intro into that market would be to really study what that person is doing and that's not anything revolutionary. That's just something really pragmatic that works. That's what I do.

Earlier, about a year and a half ago, I moved into the Michigan market in West Michigan. I'd done most of my investing in Florida, so it was a totally different market, so the first thing I did when I wanted to start moving into that Michigan market was I found the individual who'd wholesaled the most properties there over the last two years and really started developing a relationship with them, so that would be step one no matter what you're doing and no matter what the end strategy is, it's definitely lock down, identify, and start cultivating a relationship with whoever that rock star wholesaler, rehabber, house flipper is in that market. Does that make sense, Jim?

Jim: Yeah, absolutely. How did you go about finding a wholesaler because that would be a difficult ... Because you can't google wholesaler, right? Real estate wholesaler? Nothing's going to come up.

Matt: That's true.

Jim: How would you go about finding that guy?

Matt: I would do a couple different things. I would try Google, not necessarily for wholesaler, but I would look up, let's say you were going into Dayton, Ohio. Let's just pick a market out of our hat. I would type in Dayton real estate investment, Dayton real estate investor, Dayton real estate investing, Dayton wholesale properties, Dayton property wholesaler, Dayton property flipper. Every kind of search term I could think up that would bring the results of somebody or some company that's in business there in that market. I'd start compiling a list of those, and you'll see very quickly two or three of those people even though there'll be a lot of returns, two or three of those people or companies will rise to the top and you'll know who the top investors are in that area, at least from a marketing perspective.

Then you can also go on Craigslist. You can also use county records to search for names in a specific geographic area that keep showing up as a multiple buyer and many times that will be a wholesaler or an investor, too, so those are all different ways, pretty much free ways that you can start to locate that top investor or that top wholesaler, and that's just a window to that market for you. That shows you, "Hey, this is somebody who's doing a ton of deals. There must be something to these types of properties and these types of areas on this type of exit strategy" because you see somebody else having success with it.

The first thing I would think of is don't reinvent the wheel. If I move into a new market or I'm starting a new business I don't know anything about, do I want to start it from the ground up with no knowledge or do I want to essentially copy somebody else or emulate somebody else who's already successful? It always makes more sense to find somebody who already has a proven successful method and then just replicate that. That makes sense, right?

That's the first thing I would do, so develop a relationship with somebody like that. Study their model. Educate yourself. A lot of people will get stuck studying courses and studying books and studying trainings and that's great, and going on webinars. I'm a big proponent of education. I think that's great and I think we should do that, but that's no substitute for finding somebody who's in the market and really doing deals and really digging into their business and seeing how they're do it. That's the first step.

The next step would be after you've figured out who that person is, you've developed the relationship, you've studied their model, develop the relationship to the point now where you can go to that wholesaler and say, "Look, I'm developing some leads for cash buyers that want to buy investment properties and I think your properties and the kind of properties you wholesale would be perfect for some of these buyer leads that I'm creating. Would you mind if I took some of your properties and marketed them? They're your properties, obviously. I'm not trying to change anything about what you do, but you tell me what you're trying to wholesale those properties for. Can I have your permission to take some of those properties, create pro formas, maybe even create some marketing materials to show those to my buyers, bring those buyers to you, and make a cut of that deal? Would that work for you?"

Most of those wholesalers are going to say yes unless you're not presenting yourself the right way. Most people, if you tell them, "I've got buyers for your properties. Can I bring you buyers?" most of those wholesalers will say yes. Most of those people want you to bring their buyers because you're making their job easy.

That'd be the next step is getting their permission to market the properties in some way so now instead of having to go out and make your own supply, instead of having to make a bunch of MLS offers or go to the option or any of these other myriad of ways you can create your own property lead, you now basically, through creating the right relationship, you've bought yourself into an ongoing source of property leads that you can then market, but you cut yourself out of having to put down earnest deposits and having to lock down properties on your own, which can sometimes be more expensive and very hard to do with no money and no budget, so you've worked yourself into a system of property leads now that you can market.

That'd be the next step is really locking down and getting permission from them to take those properties and market, and then obviously, the next step is going to be learning how to market those properties and starting to find investor buyers that would be interested in those types of properties.

How to generate buyer leads, how do you find cash buyers, and off the top of my head, I can think of four or five different ways that you can do it very low cost or no cost.

One is simple networking. Just going to real estate investor associations and meeting investors, people that are already buying properties, asking them what they're buying, figuring out what their criteria is, and seeing if that matches up with the deal flow that you've got from your wholesaler partner, seeing if there's a match there between those buyers and the product that you have.

Another way would be to utilize social networks, and I won't go into all of this, but when you and I talked at one other point, we talked about the system that I created with Kevin Harrington from Shark Tank and that's called Internet Real Estate Tycoon. In that system, we teach how to use Facebook and how to use YouTube videos and how to rank your business on Google to generate leads for distressed sellers and for cash buyers and to have those leads coming in on autopilot. There's a lot of ways you can do that...

There's a lot of ways you can do that really, really inexpensively, so if you're going to do it with no budget whatsoever, you need to pay for it in sweat equity and do it yourself, but it's very possible to do it. If you drop me in the middle of somewhere with no money and said, "Generate leads for buyers and sellers with zero budget," it would probably be networking and these free real estate sources that I'm talking about which we teach in Internet Real Estate

Tycoon, so that'd be another way, and then really learning how to market these.

Once you start generating some buyer leads and you're starting to talk to some of these investor buyers, you need to be able to correctly convey the information about these properties. Why are these properties good? "Mr. Buyer, I've got four or five properties I'm selling right now that I'd be willing to wholesale you that are great investment properties. Two of them are great cash flow investment properties. You can buy them for 60K apiece, put about 20 into them, and rent them out, and they'll make you a 9 or 10 or 11% cap rate as rentals, so they're great buy and hold properties. These other two that I have would be great buy, fix, and flip properties. You could buy them for 100,000, put about 20 to 30 into them, and sell them for about a $20,000 net profit; after closing, after all commissions are paid, about a $20,000 net profit, and that's what these properties would do."

Being able to speak to people like that, Jim, and correctly portray. Not just, "Hey, this is a good property. You should buy it," but "This is a good property. Here's why it's good. Here is what I would do with it. Here's how it would perform," and that really explains to that buyer why they would want to do business with you. I'm sure you, Jim, you've done real estate…

You can't paint the picture. If you just say, and I have people coming to me all the time because we buy a lot of properties nationwide, so I have new sellers coming to me all the time marketing their properties and saying, "Hey, these are fantastic properties. Let me know what you'd like to offer on them," and they don't give me any info about the properties. They don't tell me anything about them.

I'm always going to do my due diligence, but when a seller comes to me trying to market properties, I want them to come with at least a decent amount of information about what they would do with it. I want to know that they're a sophisticated investor and aren't just bringing me something they found anywhere, that they actually analyze that property. I want them to come and say, "You can buy it for this much, put this much into it, and I'd recommend renting it like this and it would be this percentage cash flow monthly and this kind of cap rate." I want to know numbers of how that's actually going to perform.

Marketing is such a big piece of it and I think a lot of beginning wholesalers and people that start out in the business, they really rely on means that don't really give you the true value of the property and they convey it in a way that doesn't explain to people what the exit process is and what the exit strategy is on a property, so you need to be able to do that. Educate yourself. Have pro formas. Have pictures, have pro formas. Have real numbers and convey it like a real investor.

"If I was buying this property, here's what I would do with it. I would do this and this and this, and then I would make this much on a sale. This would be my net profit." Really spell it out for them, A, B, C, all the way to Z, of exactly how this property will perform and how it would do what you're saying it's going to do, how that looks. That's a real benefit to investors when you're trying to market to them, so that would be the next step.

After you have found the investor in your market, after you've developed a relationship with them, after you've gotten their permission to market their properties, and then you've gone out and generated some buyer leads, whether it's through networking at associations or online marketing or reaching out in some other lead generation way, you then really study the numbers, match those buyers up with those properties. Tell them why these properties are good.

Really spell it out for them and show them how this property makes money, and then only at that point if you have the wrong prospect who wasn't really a cash buyer, only at that point will they not want to do business with you because you've made it easy for them to do business with you. You've made it easy for the wholesaler whose properties you're marketing to do business with you because you're training buyers the right way as you bring them, and so everybody's happy.

The wholesaler makes money, the end buyer makes money when they flip that property or when they rent that property, and you make money because you were the conduit for that good deal, and being the conduit can happen with very little money and really, very little expertise if you approach it the right way.

I guess that's really what I would do, Jim. If you drop me off in the middle of a market and said, "Make money," it would be make a few key relationships like that and put a few co-wholesale deals together and make 5 grand, 10 grand. Start to generate some profits like that, and then eventually parlay that into locking up your own deals and starting to make bigger spreads on wholesale flips, eventually into rehabbing, and then eventually into what all investors want to be doing eventually which is buy and hold and living off a passive income, right?

Jim: Yeah, right. Let me ask you, when you said West Michigan. I won't ask you about that particular area, but if you were looking to go for an area somewhere else in the country, why would you pick a specific ... Is it because of the after repaired value price? Was it about pricing? Was it about demographic? What would you be looking for in a market?

Matt: Sure, so all of those that you mentioned are good reasons. If you can find them, all of those are good reasons to move into a market if it's different than what you can get in your own home market. For me, I moved into the West Michigan market because the Florida prices had started to creep up to a point where I could not get the rental return that I wanted to get in Florida, and the rental returns that a lot of my investors who invest with me and buy properties through me had come to expect. A lot of hedge funds had come in over the last couple years. A lot of international buyers and prices are still decent. There are still some values in Florida, but I wasn't getting some of these 10, 11, and 12%, really strong returns at cap rates that I was getting down there.

I went out to identify different markets, markets that would still provide those types of cap rates with a similar type of investment, and Michigan, West Michigan, not Detroit. I'm a little scared of Detroit still, but Michigan, Indiana, Ohio. Those three states have a lot of really good cash flow markets, and so that's why I moved into Michigan and now those other markets I've mentioned, too, because I can get really good high cap rate, good cash flow properties there.

Jim: This was more about who you're selling your properties to is what your end investor, what the cap rates still get on their long-term rentals. Is that what I'm gathering?

Matt: Yeah, it was, and also because it's what I wanted in my own personal portfolio, so yeah, it was kind of determined by both of those: A desire to diversify for my own personal holdings and also my buyers that wanted a particular type of return. I need to continue to go to good markets that will provide those returns.

Yeah, and once you get a few of those deals done and have a little bit of a budget to work with, then you can choose a lot of different ways to move forward. You can invest a little bit in some direct mail for lead generation or you can do some paid type of lead generation on the internet. There's a lot of different ways you can move forward and generate leads once you have those first few deals done, but that's the best way I can think of to really get those deals done if you honestly had no money and were starting at ground zero, and I think you could get a few deals done like that and then start to build the budget that could grow your business and scale it up.

Matt's Productivity Tip:

Yeah, absolutely. Every morning I do this thing that I'm sure no one's ever done before, and it's an incredibly new concept. It's called four cups of coffee at once, and you down it as quick as you can, and ... No, I'm just kidding. I'm just kidding, but I do that sometimes.

I do over-caffeinate every once in a while, but no, to answer your question seriously, if I got it down to one tip or one tool that

I use that's helped me more than anything, especially in the last year or so as we really made a commitment to taking our business even up to that next level, and this is pretty simple and it won't be revolutionary, but it's really just taking the time to, for lack of a better term, it's taking the time to breathe before you start something.

Every Sunday I usually look at the next week that I have planned out, and it's just a few minutes. Maybe 5 or 10 minutes, I look at what's on the schedule for that next week and I prepare my mind for that week. I remind myself of what I'm trying to accomplish that week. I remind myself of how those things fit into my larger goals, whatever my main larger yearly goals are, how those fit in. I double check them to make sure they're in alignment with those goals, and then every day when I wake up in the morning, before I start making phone calls, before I answer email, before I record any podcasts or do anything that I do, before I sign any contracts, anything like that, I take a few minutes to think about the day. Sometimes it's only 2 or 3 minutes, but it could be some people would call it their time of prayer. Some people would call it a time of meditation. Some people call it just sitting out on the back porch with a cup of coffee in silence.

That's my secret, man. When I started doing that, I used to wake up in the morning, a phone in each hand and checking 12 emails and recording 5 trainings and doing this and that and running around to houses. I found that when I stopped and really took the time to just have a little quiet time in the morning of reflection, whether you're thinking and focused on business or just not focusing on anything, just focusing on being there before you really get in the hustle and bustle, that's made an amazing impact for me.

Really, what it's served for me is that every morning I touch back for just a minute with what it is I'm trying to accomplish in my life. I think sometimes we get so busy and we get so caught up in our goal, and so many of us, people listening to this or reading this, many are entrepreneurs and type A personalities and we go, go, go all the time, and we have an ability to short-circuit ourselves when we run like that without touching back to what the goal is.

Really, that time in the morning for me, that time on Sunday night, and that time every morning at the start of my day, it's just a time to quickly have a touch back to what's the goal, what are we trying to accomplish overall here from a long-term perspective? Are the things that we're doing today and are the things that we're doing this week right now in line with those goals and going to push us forward to the accomplishment of those goals? That's really it, man. It's not much of a secret, but it's really being conscious of what we're [crosstalk 00:21:21] focus there.

It's hard. It's hard to take the time to do it, too. It's hard to discipline ourselves to take the time to do it sometimes. We'll make all these elaborate business plans, but sometimes we don't make these plans with just life. For me, it's a time to remember that whatever business I'm doing that day is secondary in my life to my family and to my faith and to other things that, honestly, are way more important than money and way more important than business, so for me it's a time of priority, too. It's a time to sit down and say, "OK, my daughter's healthy. My wife loves me. I'm blessed with a great family. I have my needs met."

Are there things that I want to accomplish, goals I want to do and things I want to get out there and get done? Of course. Of course they are, but I'm a blessed man and I use that opportunity to remember and to prioritize what's important in my life. I think when you start the day like that ... When you start your week and you start your days like that reminding yourself what's important, I think it helps everything throughout that day and throughout that week flow in line. If something pops up and we as entrepreneurs see opportunities everywhere ... If something pops up that's a great opportunity that doesn't fit in with what we're trying to accomplish long-term, touching back every day like that helps us realize that.

It helps us realize that even though this is something really cool and something fun and something that makes a little bit of money, this is not the best use of my skills to accomplish my long-term goals, so it's really about keeping those goals in front of you and taking a couple minutes every morning to realize where it is that you're going to make sure that you don't veer off path because we have a tendency to do that as entrepreneurs. I've got attention deficit disorder, so I can go way off the rails really, really quick if I don't continually remind myself on why I'm doing what I'm doing.

To get a free copy of Matt's book and see his free training videos

Visit: www.GetOnTheInside.com

Alan Cowgill

Alan is an author, national speaker, and a private lending consultant. He's regularly featured in newspaper articles about purchasing real estate through private lenders.

He's been in three national infomercials. He's published in two books titled, Walking With the Wise in Real Estate, and Walking With the Wise Entrepreneur, with people like Donald Trump and Chuck Norris, who are also featured in those books.

Alan started his real estate career in 1995, so he's been in the real estate business for almost two decades. In 2011 he quit his job to become a full time real estate investor. He's created systems to show you how to buy five to seven house a month and has done hundreds of real estate transactions

Alan's Answer:

What I would do first is what I did do. I started out with education. A foundation of this business. I learned early on is education and I didn't have any money. I was broke. I was living in a little dinky two-bedroom apartment, and couldn't pay all my bills.

In fact, what I was living through at the time, I had this old beat up car that needed to have some money put into it, but I didn't have the money to do it, and I put that on the back burner because I was too busy paying other bills. One night on a first date that car paid me back.

I pulled up in front of this apartment complex, take this lady, walk her up to her door from our first date, and half way up to the door I turned around and looked, and my car had burst into flames. It hadn't had any maintenance work on the thing. Pretty embarrassing. That's back when I was working a j-o-b.

I've got a quarter century in corporate America before I got into real estate. I realized early on that I needed to change my life, and I saw an infomercial on real estate, and I thought, "You know, I can do this." I got the system and started to study the system. I start out with education. It literally changed the rest of my life.

I didn't have any money like I said, so I started to go to the library and get books on real estate. Joined the local REIA group, real estate investor group. I didn't even know they existed til I saw an ad in the paper. I joined that group, eventually became a director on there.

I started to purchase home study systems, go to Saturday workshops that they would have in the area. Then eventually went to boot camps, and I would be on teleseminars listening to folks, now we've got webinars. The foundation was the education. My dad had told me once, he said, "Two things will change your life, what you read and who you meet."

I started out on what you read on real estate to change my life. Then on the who you meet part of it, I realized that for me to really leap from my business is I paid for the who you meet. Once I got some money coming in I was able to join mentoring programs, coaching programs, $15,000 a year coaching program, and things like that. That helped on the foundation.

One of the things while I was going through all this education is I had to pick what element, I call it the model, of real estate, that I wanted to be in. There's commercial and residential, but there's a number of different ways to make money in real estate. On the commercial side you've got storage units and office buildings and strip malls and multi-units, and large apartment complexes.

You can focus on one of those and become wealthy. If you're on the residential stuff side you could do ugly houses which are what I do or pretty houses, and you can have rentals. One of the things, I had to fare it out when I was getting started was which element of this business, or which model I wanted to be in.

The other thing I did early, early on is I put down a list of goals. I had written goals. They have this saying that goes around, it might be an urban legend, but they say that someone took a study of the senior class at Yale University at one point in time and found out that 3% had written goals. They came back and reviewed that class 20 years later and found out that the 3% had more money than the rest of the class combined.

I don't know if it's true or not, but the thing of it is, goals work for me. What I did was, I went out to K-Mart, and I bought a cork board, and I nailed it to the wall in the rental that I was in. I didn't own a house, I was living in a rental unit. I nailed to the wall with my goals, and I had short term goals and long term goals.

Then what happened was things started to click for me. I would write the word victory after those goals when I achieved them. It would say, "Buy a multi-unit apartment complex." When I did then I wrote the word victory. That made a tremendous difference in my life.

You talked about marketing strategies and things like that. There's four parts of a real estate deal at the very top level. Number 1 is you've got to find the property. Number 2 is you've got to fund it. Number 3 is you fix it. Number 4 is you flip is. That's a basic for anything that I just mentioned there a little bit ago about different elements of this business.

The front end piece of this business is finding and the marketing is the key on that. You have to open up the front end piece of your business. What I find from coaching student's that we've got, that I coach, one of the biggest errors that they make is exactly that ailment right there Jim. I'm very tickled that you brought that up because that can help so many folks.

They have to open up the front end piece of their business. I saw something once that made an impact on me. Someone had done a study of 30 different ways to market for real estate, putting up signs or sending out fliers or newspaper ads or different ways. What happened was there wasn't, on the list I saw, there wasn't a magic bullet if you will, that when you look down thought that list of 30 different ways to market, each one of them would have one or two, maybe three properties that they had got over that period of time.

What that told me was that I really needed to focus on a lot of different ways to market. There is some that I found over time really work pretty good in the area I'm in is signs. You put up signs. I like to by bandit signs, get the ones with the yellow background and black letters, put those up. Those do work well. Mailings, to mail to different folks. There's a lot of different ways, websites, and items like that.

One of the things I've got is I created my own system to where I could get a list of realtors in a 50 mile radius of where I live, and ended up with 314 realtors, and then I could set up a campaign to where I would email them once a month. I'd have 14 emails. The first couple months I'd mail a couple extra times. Set up a relationship with the realtor to where they would feed me deals.

The other thing that you mentioned early on was where I have a system to buy five to seven houses a month and I set that up with a person that just got his real estate license. I had been looking for a way to dial in REO's; real estate's owned by banks. What happened was he was at a closing with me, and was there to pick up the check. He had just got his license, and this was the second closing he'd ever been to. He asked me if he could show me properties, and I agreed to it.

Working with him and my vision of what to do, I set up a system to where I could take a look at six to ten properties every week. What would happen was he would do all the research. He would figure out the properties on the market, and pick me up on a Friday afternoon, and from 1:30 to 4:30 we'd drive around and I'd look at these properties and make offers on every single one of them.

If I didn't care for the property, it was too small or something, I'd just make a low ball effort that since I spent my time and effort to do that, I'd go ahead and make an offer. What happened in that system was I'd submit the offers. Let's say we have six offers the first week, I'd submit them, and six offers the next week, submit those. By the end of the month I had 24 offers.

Typically all those offers initially would get rejected, but here's the magic in what I created. I resubmitted the same offers on the 20th of every month. You might say, "Why'd you pick the 20th?" A couple reasons. One it's my son's birthday. He's born on the 20th of April, so it's an easy day for me to remember. Also, banks tend to cough up properties end of the month, end of the quarter, end of the fiscal year.

By putting in the follow up offers month after month after month, I would be in the sweet spot where they would maybe consider my offer while I would continue to make offers on these properties that I've already done my due diligence on. What I found was a couple things. One is a lot of new real estate investors, what they'll do is they'll make an offer, they get turned down, and they quit. What I did was not quit.

I found that in months four, five, six, seven, and beyond that these banks would sell me the house to the tune of five to seven properties a month minimum.

All MLS. 100% MLS. What had happened was I'd set this system up to make offers. One of the things you're talking about is marketing on the front end piece of the business. What I find anemic in my new real estate investors is this front end piece of the business that you're talking about. They don't have enough coming across their desk, and on the ones they do have coming across their desk, they don't have the courage many times to make the offer.

The reason they don't make the offer is because they don't have the money to buy it if it did come through. For an example, on those 24 offers I make every month, if they all come through I have a party because I've got the money to fund the deals. If someone out there gets one offer, two offers accepted, many times they don't have the money to fund the deals.

What happened to me was along the way I learned about private money. That's the second part of those big four that I gave you, the find, fund, fix, and flip. Having private money made all the difference to me. What happened to me early on was I was able to figure out what private money was all about.

In fact, to be honest with you Jim when I started out, I thought hard money and private money were the same things. Actually, they're distinctly different.

Hard money lender, they set a bunch of rough rules with real estate investors where you've got to pay them back in 12 months, and you can't rent the place out once you fix it up. When you got to closing to buy they allocate some money for you to rehab the property, but they don't give it to you. You have to dig into your pocket a second time. First time is a down payment when you go to closing. Mine charged me 15%.

Then they would hold this money back to rehab. What would happen is I'd have to dig into my own pocket to start the demolition work, and bring the property up to a certain level, and then I'd call up my hard money lender, and I'd ask them, I'd say, "I'm ready to get that rehab money", and what they would do, because they held it back. They escrowed the money, and they would send in an appraiser that I paid for. If I did what I said, put my own money into it then they would start releasing some of the money. They call it draws.

They would give me one, two, or three draws depending on the deal. That was pretty expensive on putting the money down on a down payment. Let's take a simple example here of a $100,000 loan. $100,000 at 15%, that's $15,000 that you got to take into closing. That was a wheelbarrow of money for me.

It was a struggle, and then I had to dig into my pocket a second time, like I said, for the rehab, so I could start getting some of the fix up money. What happened to me was I was able to crack the code on private money. I found a way to do it. Along the way I wanted to make sure I was following all the legal aspects of private money, and I hired an attorney.

I gave him a project to research my state, and then when I began teaching, research the whole United States and Canada too. One day he called me up, and he said, "Hey Alan I'm done with the project. I just want to thank you though", and I said, "Why's that?" He said, "Well, I'm moving into my new house, and you bought it."

I got to tell you Jim that's not what you want to hear from any attorney. I'll tell you what, it had paid off for me because in reality, I'm probably the nation's leading expert on private money and how to do it and be safe with the FCC. My attorney research every single state in the United States and like I said and Canada, and so that gave me the wherewithal to be able to teach it, and teach people how to not only get private money, but to be safe.

Let me share something with you if you've got a second. One of the things I'm really proud about is, as you know, I hold a four day event on how to acquire private money. I've been doing it since 2004. In my very first event I set the stage to where my students could attract private money overnight. To be honest with you, I thought it would work, but until you actually see 175 students go out and implement what you ask you don't know how it's going to turn out. The results were amazing.

In that first event we raised $4 million in less than 24 hours, and that's their money. That's money they use to go fund a real estate deals. I had one guy quit his job right after the boot camp because he had so much money, and he was ready to move on as a full time real estate investor. In fact I see it happen a number of times in the events.

As you and I are speaking right now, I hold about 3 events a year, and since 2004 we've raised over a half a billion dollars in the first 24 hours of my events.

We're working our way toward a billion. It's been incredible. Hand and hand in that is the securities and exchange commission. The good news is that the rules for us as real estate investors are incredibly simple to follow when it comes to the FCC.

The problem is they're hard to find. There wasn't anybody teaching it when I started to teach it. What I do is not only teach people how to amass private money like I just talked about, but I also teach them to do it safely with the FCC. Folk and folks got to have it. They love it. In fact it's like a sporting event. If you go watch a football game or a baseball game, there's not only the fundamentals of the game. I went out for high school football, my coach would teach me to block, I was an offensive defensive guard. He would teach me how to block and tackle and play the position.

What he also did was hand me a rule book. The rule book said if you're carrying the ball, and it goes 10 yards you get first down. If you're carrying the ball, and you go across the goal line you get a touchdown. It's the same with private lending. I teach people the fundamentals of how to acquire private money and how to manage the money with private lenders. Also I give them the rule book on how to do it and how to do it safely, so they can sleep at night.

I know I ran through a lot of different items. Starts back with the education, goes to goal setting, goes to picking your model, and then the four elements of a real estate deal, the find, fund, flip, fix piece of it. You got to open the front end piece of your business with your marketing. I gave you a number of different scenarios there.

That's all the events combined. In every event we raise multimillion of dollars at the event in 24 hours, and it's a 4 day event. If folks would like to learn more on what I do Jim, they could go to www.privatelendingmadeeasy.com. Those words are all just spelled out, privatelendingmadeeasy.com. I've got 35 e-coaching lessons there that they could grab.

Every week I send them another e-coaching lesson. It's free and could get them started, and it covers a lot of the things you and I been talking about.

Alan's Productivity Tip:

System. I'm a systems guy. The backbone of my systems are check lists. I gave you a system at the very top level on how to buy five to seven properties a month. In order to do that I had to have a system. That's the key to this. Focus on a system, you got to get up every day, running and making sure you're focused on what you want to do. A lot of it comes back to what you're talking about on marketing, and what you're asking me to talk about because without that marketing, without opening up the front end piece of the business, you're dead on making offers because you don't have anything to make offers on.

The other piece is having knowledge where you get into the funding piece of it. Obviously I would have private lenders. In fact, I can't imagine somebody listening to this right now that doesn't have private lenders. Many of them are begging for money to make, or messing around with hard money lenders which will bleed you dry. You got private lenders, and all those rules change because you get to set the rule. That's the difference between anything else. If you're getting money from any place else they're setting the rules. If you get money through private lenders, private individuals that have massed some money, then you get to set the rules.

Think about having that second big item on funding, and rather than having somebody else set rules you got to follow, you can set your own rules. To answer on productivity, habit, you got to be focused, you got to be knowledgeable, and you got to have systems.

Alan holds a 4-day private money seminar that is not to be missed. For more information on Alan and to get his free video training on private money visit: www.privatelendingmadeeasy.com

Andrew Cordle

Andrew is a seasoned investor with over 10 years' experience. This guy has flipped over 100 rehabs in just 1 year alone. He is a nationally recognized speaker and educator. His passion is helping people find their purpose. In 2013, he celebrated a groundbreaking strategic alliance with Home Depot, where they helped investors save thousands of dollars on their rehab budgets. You can go to his web site to ask him more about that.

Andrew has flipped hundreds of homes in multiple states and tours the country, sharing his vast wealth of knowledge with investors at all experience levels; from beginners to advanced investors, this guy is teaching you how to do things. Andrew loves to teach to investors how to flip houses and mentors a small group of select investors who have had great success at applying his proven systems.

Andrew's Answer:

That's a great question and I broke it down into 2 phases for us here. Number 1, what would I do different if I started over from scratch? I see a lot of investors that make a lot of the same mistakes. It's amazing how many investors come into the market and it seems like so many of them made the same mistake, which I made that mistake, as well. Fortunately, I was able to recover from it, but I see a lot of them that are just never able to recover from it. I'm going to talk a little bit about that.

I'm also going to break into marketing and I'm going to share with you some really cool insight and some marketing strategies that our companies use to find hundreds and hundreds of deals that probably nobody else has actually really mentioned here on this conversation we having going on, this call we have going on. First let me ask you the first one which is what would I do starting over from scratch?

I think that answer is this. You have to figure out before you jump into this thing of real estate investing, you have to figure out your strategy. Your strategy may be different from my strategy. That's the great thing about real estate investing is that strategies are different. The main mistake that beginner investors I see that are making a mistake, is they don't know where they're headed with this investing. They're excited, they want to get into it, they're anxious to get into it. They attend a local REIA or a club where they get into a little bit of information and then boom, they just make the first deal.

They don't know where they're really headed in their real estate career. I think if they would take a moment and take a step back and understand okay, this is where I'm at financially in my life and that's where I want to be financially in my life. This is a strategy and this is where I'm going to go with real estate investing so that every investment has a purpose. Every house now is a building block getting you to the finish line. It's like having a race and you have a starting point which is where you're at right now and then you have a finish line.

Every house that you do, every investment you make should be going down that same path of getting to that finish line. If you'll do that and if you'll get into the right strategy because Jim, you know as much as anybody a lot of times these real estate investors will get into, I'm sure you've seen it, as well, where these investors get into shiny objects syndrome and every time they turn around, they're chasing another rabbit here and they're chasing another rabbit here and there's 13 ways to do this and there's 5 ways to do this. All those things work.

That's the thing. All of these different, if you will, tactics work; lease option, whole sale, subject to, buy-fix-sell, commercial. They all have value and they all work, but I've never really seen anybody be a master of everything. Normally, we find those successful investors and they know what they're doing. I'm a buy-fix-sell guy. I think you are, too, Jim. I'm a buy-fix-sell guy, so that's what I focus on. I hammer buy-fix-sell, buy-fix-sell. I don't get side-tracked with oh, here's a really cool, shiny subject to house over here. Let me go play with this for a little bit.

When those subject deals come in, because that's not in my strategy, I don't get sidetracked by it and I don't go try to be all things to all real estate transactions. I may kick it off to another investor of mine. I may sell it off for a thousand bucks over here, but I don't get side-tracked with it. I have my strategy. I stick with it and that's what's made me successful over the length of investing is I know where I'm headed and I know where I want to be. That's the strategy. There's a follow up to this answer, is #1, obviously, know your strategy and #2, you have to know your tactic, which is a little bit what I was talking about there.

I don't get side-tracked with all these different tactics of commercials and commercial deals and subject to and lease. Every time you turn around there's another, if you will, shiny object that's coming out. All of them like I said and probably you can make money off of, but I really focus on what I do, how I do it. I know my tactic. I know my strategy. I know where I'm headed and I know the tactics I'm going to use to help me get there. I think if I could start all the way over again, I would shave several years off of my investing career by every deal that came in if I knew it had a purpose from the beginning.

I know at the beginning, for several years every deal that came along I was doing versus having a full-on strategy, knowing my tactic and applying those tactics into my strategy to help me get to the end goal. I think that was the #1 thing that I would do. As you mentioned, Jim, I travel around, speaking constantly with investors and groups of investors and students that we work with. That's the biggest thing I see. If I sit down and talk to an investor or a potential investor and say, "Hey, where are you at with your investing career?" They're like, "Oh, I'm doing 2 flips."

I'm not asking you what you're doing right now. I'm trying to get to where are you headed with this thing and they're like, "Oh, I'll do the next deal as it comes along." I think that's a big mistake that I see with investors nowadays. Lastly, to end this thing, Jim, if

I gave you an example here, it would be say if I wanted to open up a Subway franchise.

If I wanted to open a Subway franchise and let's say that I want to go to a bank to get my small business loan, right, my SBA loan, when I go in there to the bank, one of the very first things that small business administrator is going to ask me for; you know what the very first thing they're going to ask me for? It's hey, Andrew, I need to see your full business plan. They want to make sure that I have a plan, I have an attack, and I have a strategy on how I'm going to make this Subway successful. Literally, to get an SBA loan, you have to give them a detailed business plan.

If you ask real estate investors across the nation hey, can I see your business plan where you're showing me your growth and how you're going to actually take this from a mom and pop, 1-house company into a company that you're doing 10, 12, 15 houses a year, none of them have business plans. Investors just don't know where they're headed as they get into this business.

Take some time, figure out your strategy, know your approach, create your business plan, figure out your tactic, and know your tactic of real estate investing. Don't try to be all things to all houses. You do what you do, whichever tactic you want, man, just be successful at that and you'll be surprised at how fast you'll start making money in this industry.

Jim: Yeah, I know. I think you make a good point. I think a lot of us as entrepreneurs have that shiny object syndrome and even students that come into my network, they have that. They're the jack of all trades, master of nothing, right? They haven't mastered any one thing because they try to learn it all. All of these strategies work, right; as you say, whether you're doing rehabs or whole sale or lease options, subject to. We all know these. Guys do it all over the country, have been doing it for years, all the way through the ups, the downs. They work.

You're right, not one guy you will find that's achieving a high level in this industry is doing all of them, nobody.

Andrew: Nobody. That's exactly right. If someone could do a survey and say let's go find all the highly successful investors that are out there in real estate investing and let's pinpoint how many approaches or how many tactics they're doing, you're not doing to find … For me, I guess you could say I do 2; I do buy-fix-sell and I do buy-fix-hold of single-family homes. I don't even waver from that. If I do buy-fix-hold single family homes, I don't go turn around and just say all of a sudden I'm going to go buy a 12-plex now because I understand the rental market.

Guess what? A single family home rental and a 12-plex, those are 2 different types of rental properties. You can't just be the jack of all trades. I'll give you a quick example here. I was just with one of my coaching students and they'd just signed up. I was sitting down with them and I actually flew to where they were. We were looking at a bunch of their properties. He was driving around and I was coaching him for the day. He asked me ... I was talking about his background and he said right now, I just signed up for your coaching program.

I was excited. This guy was a smart guy and I was like, "This is going to be great. You'll be a good student." I was working with him. All of a sudden in the car, he was like, "Okay, well I got your coaching program, I've also signed up for multifamily down in Texas and a hotel investing in New Hampshire" or something. I'm like, "Dude." First of all, you just dropped 75 thousand dollars and do you understand the chances of you being successful at all 3 of those at the exact same time? That's like being an IT person, a controller and a COO all at the same time. They just don't fit together. You know what I mean.

That's the biggest thing. I would say just focus on the strategy. It's a race. You've got to have a starting point and a finish line. Know where your finish line is. Real estate is just the vehicle that gets us to where we're trying to go. We can replace real estate with franchises. We could replace real estate with the stock market or whatever. That's just the vehicle that helps us get to the end goal, but if you don't know your end goal, it's amazing to see how many people get in real estate and get out of real estate, get in real estate and then get out of real estate because they don't know where they're headed.

I'm going to give you some advice; not advice but let me give you my strategy here that I don't really share with anybody. This is very, very sacred to me, but as we were talking, I wanted to share this with some of your people that are going to be listening to this and that's it. When it comes to marketing, I was doing the 10 houses at a time, right? I've got 10 flips going on at a time, 12 flips at a time going on and I just couldn't get my inventory fast enough. I was doing all the things that everyone does; the bandit signs, the yellow letters, the horsey letters, the purple paper. Everybody's doing this.

We're all through doing the same thing. I just couldn't really get enough inventory as I was building this big machine of buy, fix and sell. I was successful at the time. I had some money, so I said you know what I'm going to do? I'm going to hire a legitimate chief marketing officer for my company and I don't want them to have a real estate background. I want someone who is a legitimate, graduated with a marketing degree that has worked with large companies that has a different perspective than every single real estate investor.

No matter what guru I would go to, no matter what group I would go to, it was all the same thing. You've got to have bandit signs, you've got to put them in rotation, and you've got to hit them every other Saturday. You should go make your rounds. It's all through a lot of the same things with a different twist on it. I went out and I hired this marketing director, for well over 6-figure salary I hired this guy. He had worked with Pepsi-Cola, Buffalo Wild Wings, with national programs with them. I hired him and he's a graduate from Ohio State with a marketing degree.

I said look, take the first 30, 60 days or so in the company and look at all of our marketing, go through everything, see what we do and then come back to me. Tell me what we should do different. I'll never forget. He comes back to my office after about a week or so, 2 weeks. He said let me ask you a question. I need to ask you about your in-bound marketing. I said okay, in-bound marketing. I like where this is headed. I'm a big fan of inbound marketing. His name is Eddie. I've been a big fan of inbound marketing, but you know what? Let's hold that question and let's come back to another one.

He's like, "Tell me about outbound marketing then. Tell me about your outbound strategy." I could see this was going to go nowhere because now all of a sudden he's speaking marketing lingo which I don't know. I know real estate lingo, but I don't know marketing lingo. I said, Eddie, I'm going to be honest with you. I have no idea what inbound marketing is or outbound marketing. I don't know what either one of those are. This is where my business changed with the amount of houses that I was getting.

That was we changed how we were doing our marketing strategy. Most real estate investors are strictly outbound marketing, outbound marketing, outbound marketing. Outbound marketing defined basically is just say, it's interruption-based marketing. Outbound marketing would be a billboard. You're driving to work, you don't wake up one day and say I want see how many billboards I can read today. You wake up, you're driving to work and you see a billboard which then provides a thought which then you may be able to go buy something. That's interruption-based.

Direct mail, that's interruption-based marketing. Someone's getting the mail, they're going through it. You send them a letter to buy their house. It's interruption-based. Inbound marketing is really where society as a whole is heading. Inbound marketing, the difference of that is inbound is going to be you provide relative information for your customer and allow your customer to make a decision. We began to switch up and we still do outbound marketing, but we began to dive heavy into inbound marketing. Inbound marketing means we would start a blog in our local area.

To give you guys an example here, if you in your local area Googles, "I'm losing my house, what do I do," or a key phrase that someone that was going through foreclosure would be typing in "I'm 30 days behind mortgage, what's next?" We began to write blogs with those key phrases inside of it, SBO key phrases and all of a sudden our area over time and we were using a free blog, very, very generic. We didn't have a professional designer come and design it. It was a very homemade blog and we wanted that feel of local homemade presence, basically.

Now in our area if you were to Google "I'm losing my house, what do I do," you pull up our blog. It pulls up and then we provide you legitimate information and then we say hey, we're located in the area. We don't say we're trying to buy your house. Nowhere does it say I'll pay cash for your house because that's going to be outbound marketing. What I'm trying to do is provide information, allow that person to make a legitimate, thoughtful decision and it was amazing how this changed our business. It's the same thing that we do, right?

Let's say that I want to buy a new TV and I'm going to buy the new 90-inch flat screen TV and I Google "Ninety-inch flat screen TV" or whatever, I don't want to go to a web site that says buy our TVs today, we'll give you a free brochure. I don't want to be bombarded with you trying to sell me your TV. I don't want to sign up. I don't want to give you all my information. I don't want to do that stuff. I'm just trying to research information right now. Once I determine through reviews and reading it and all that stuff, then we make a decision.

That's the same way that marketing works with foreclosures. We noticed that once we switched to inbound marketing, there are many, many different things that we do here. The great thing about inbound marketing, Jim, is that most of it is free. Our budget went down drastically. Here's the difference. Inbound marketing takes awhile to set up. When I saw your question, what would I do different starting over from the beginning? I'm telling you right now, it would be start my inbound marketing process. Inbound marketing takes some time to get up and going. It's like the foundation of your business.

Throughout the year, 2 years that we were doing our inbound marketing, all of a sudden we were bombarded with more phone calls than we could even manage these phone calls of people that were calling in.

We would use the blog. We would use Craigslist. We would use Facebook. Facebook marketing, I can sit here and target. Give you an example. Let's say inheritance, right? What we would do is we would go onto Facebook and we would target the word in our area, anybody that was using the word 'inheritance." Therefore, we're under the assumption that they were receiving some sort of inheritance which is now getting to be estate stuff. They need to unload a property. We would pick the word "child support" or "divorce."

What happens, we notice that all of our friends are on Facebook; 93% of America is on social media. What we would notice is that these people on social media, they were going through a divorce, right? What we didn't do, understand this, we didn't bombard them with ads like outbound marketing. We would target those people and then just talk about how to sell your house fast with no commissions. We were not sending them to this landing page that was sucking all the information out and then we'd follow up with them.

We would just provide them with information, they would click on it. It would be an article about exactly what they were dealing with. A divorce tells us there may be a chance of a house selling. We would use the divorce as a launching pad to get them into that they need to sell their house or inheritance or child support. There are all these key words that we would use there. Of course, you can target that to people that are just in your certain zip codes.

We switched our whole marketing thing, Jim, from outbound marketing, which we still do, don't get me wrong. Outbound marketing is very, very important. We still do outbound marketing, but we became an inbound marketing team, where now our calls were coming into us of people that would call and say, hey, I've been reading your blog. My husband just lost his job. We have this property and we don't know what we're going to do with it. Is there anything that you can really help us with this property?

We would. That's what we would do. We would go say, hey, let's come and meet you. The whole process starts then of sitting down and talking to them and stuff. The word that we would use a lot as getting into marketing, now you're getting into the level that I could spend hours about branding, which marketing and branding are 2 completely separate things. We created a brand in our area that we were an advocate. By branding, branding is associated feeling is what that really means.

In our area, when you heard our company name, say that you're in a foreclosure, we wanted you to have a feeling that we were an advocate trying to help you, not that we were a shark trying to take your house away.

Jim:	I would say consultative selling, right? You're basically consulting them on direction and for the right one, cool.
Andrew:	Exactly, you've got it exactly right. It's like consulting. They would call us and all of a sudden, we would say well hey look, in your situation,

here are your 4 options that you legitimately have. We would just really educate them, right? It's like an education sale. We would educate them. We wouldn't come in guns a-blazing, saying I could buy your house in 5 days and pay all cash for it and sign this contract, I'll give you a 10-dollar deposit. We came in said okay, in your current situation, here's what you're going through, here's where your house is at. I know of four different strategies that you could sell your house.

Only one of them I can help you with. The other three I can't, but here's what you could do and we would just lay it all out for them. They would say ... Most of the time, it was amazing because again, we're going to remind you, and how did they hear about us? They heard about us through education, right? The blog which is out there producing. They'd read a small article on how to save real estate commissions. How to sell your house if you're in foreclosure. They already had this trust.

We would go in these houses and I would see just like I'm sure you have, as well. You would see a stack of envelopes and you could tell that's an investor one. I could just glance at their mail and see that there's a postcard from a whole seller. I would sit in a room before they really went to those people because again, I have earned their trust; not through outbound marketing. I earned their trust through educating them, by providing them relevant information. When I sat down and talked with them, they felt like they already knew who I was. I'd never met them. I'd never seen them, but the relationship was already established.

If you've ever sat down in someone's living room, which I'm sure you have, that's one of the tough things. They're wall is up and you've got to get that wall down and get that wall down and get that wall down to close the deal. I this situation, all of a sudden, it changed and they were coming to us, asking us, you're the expert, what should I do? How should I get out of this situation? Our housing inventory exploded. That's why I did those hundreds of houses in a year. We changed our market strategy.

I say this because your question is a great question, Jim. It says if I was starting up from the beginning, what's the strategy that I would use? I would tell all of your readers, all your listeners out there that I would focus on inbound marketing, slowing build that foundation. You can do most of it absolutely for free. Build that foundation. Get the machine going. Give inbound marketing and then throw in some outbound marketing for some quick response while your inbound marketing is going. Does that make sense?

Jim: It makes perfect sense and I think that what a lot of people should take away from what you just said about the consultative selling or that approach is that the people are going to trust you automatically. When you're telling me there's 3 other options that you can do that are not me, you can go do these; these are your options, too. I can only help you with one of those. They're going to be in their heads. This guy is telling me how to not use him. I really want to see what is because I trust this guy. That's the response you get a lot and I think that's why you're probably having a lot of success with this, correct?

Andrew: Exactly. It's all relationship-built. It's all education sales, consulting sales, however you want to say that. You've just got to put yourself in their situation. These people that are going through foreclosures or divorce, the five D's if you will of the foreclosure process. Whatever that is, normally they're going through a hard time. It doesn't mean that they don't understand how to use the internet. I remember starting 10, 12 years ago into real estate. Maybe the internet wasn't as popular. Nobody was really doing Facebook marketing 12 years ago. As time has changed, so is the way that we absorb information.

As the market changes ... Just a couple days ago, I bought the newest Samsung Galaxy note 4 because I had the iPad, I had the mini iPad, I got the iPhone and now I want the new thing with a tablet. I finally switched over just a couple days ago to the Samsung Galaxy note 4 because now I can get my information quicker, faster. I don't have to have my iPhone and my mini iPad together with me. That's just the generation, the society, the culture that we live in. If you want to be successful in this, you need to learn how to communicate with the medium of which those people, your customers are using.

The best way to do that is earn their business through providing them relevant information for what they're dealing with.

Jim: It seems so easy when you say it that way, but obviously, it's definitely not the norm. That is for sure. Being in the business, talking to a lot of people, any of us that do the outbound marketing, which is what 99.9% of investors do but obviously you're doing that when you're there anyway. If you take that approach where I just buy houses cash when you're there, they get spooked. People don't like that. You will find that very easily when you go there. Here's what I can pay you.

If you're not transparent and you're not a real person to them, their either desperate or they're in a situation where they're losing their house or it's inherited and they're overwhelmed because they now got payments if there's a mortgage still. Either way, people are already freaked out in most cases and if you just go there and throw money at them; this is all I can pay, you've got to sell quick, sign here, you're going to freak them out. When you tell them their options, I think that's very powerful stuff.

Andrew: Yeah. This didn't come from me. You said it a while ago, 99% nine percent of your competition; that's the way I looked at it. The point was I was doing what all my competitors were doing, banded signs, letters, all this different stuff, but I needed more inventory. If you remember, at the beginning of the show, I told you I went and hired a high-level, 6-figure chief marketing officer and this strategy didn't come from a seminar that I heard somewhere that another real estate guru was doing, teaching everybody else.

This strategy came from a chief marketing officer that worked with Pepsi and Buffalo, all these major corporations as their marketing director. He came in and completely switched how we did marketing and said you guys are missing the point. He told me, I remember when we were having a conversation, and he said have you ever seen the movie "Back to the Future?" I'm like, "Yeah." He said, "That's where you're at." He said marketing has moved on. The mediums of which people get information has moved and you're still stuck back in the '90s. He said you need to get out of there and switch over.

I can't tell you, Jim, how much our phone once we had the foundation there, how much our phones were just ringing and ringing and ringing. The biggest thing was our outgo money because you're doing thousands of letters per month if you're really doing it and the postcards, you're doing thousands of stuff per month. All of a sudden, over time that pendulum began to swing and we just weren't spending as much money because we had so many deals from the inbound marketing.

It's a great, awesome strategy. It is a little bit high-level because you've got to understand outbound/inbound. You're actually getting almost a little bit away from real estate because now you've got to understand marketing to become successful at what you do. Sometimes, that's how business works.

Jim: Everything, every business does marketing on one level or another. If it's all going inbound, outbound, if it's direct mail or if it's word of mouth, every business is built on marketing no matter what. That's awesome. That was an awesome answer to the marketing. You're correct in saying there's been no answer like that yet. That was awesome.

Andrew's Productivity Tip:

Great question. I'm going to give you a little bit more of the technology side. I'm not going deal with so much your schedule. Everybody's a little bit different, some people are night owls, where some people are early risers. I'm a very organized person and you hit the nail on the head that you're never going to reach success without organization. I teach all these different events and seminars and it's amazing because I look at people and they're so … They have a hard time taking notes in the right order as we're teaching. Organization is key if you want to be successful and that goes in anything out there.

I use 2 apps. They're absolutely awesome. Both of them are free that you can use. I'll give them to you now. This is my command center. It's called Nozbe, N-O-Z-B-E. I don't know if you ever heard of it before, but it's called Nozbe.

Nozbe is my command center. What happens there is I can go in there and before I got on this phone call, I was on Nozbe on my new tablet, right? I can go on there and I can, obviously, create my to-do list for the day. Any time I have something that's on my mind, I'll just throw it in there in the inbox and then it allows me to click priorities, set schedules for myself, what I want to get done today, what I need to get done this week and then create side projects. If I have different employees, different so forth, web designers, bloggers, I'll create different projects.

I can then share those projects with the people that are involved in those projects. I can share it with them. We can communicate back and forth inside of it. It's absolutely … It's what I wake up and I do all throughout the day. I'm running my day-to-day operations off of Nozbe; great, great app.

I'll give you another app there. If you get really, really big and you have a lot of employees, there's another app. This won't apply as much, but there's an app called Producteev, again it's a free app. That's if you get to where you have like in the past, I've had it where I've had 25 different employees. I would use Producteev a lot. Since we've cut back on a lot of our staff, now I use Nozbe.

The last app I'll give you is an app for if you're doing the buy, fix and sales. We have a lot of projects going on. If you're doing a lot of buy, fix and sells, we use an app called Slack, S-L-A-C-K. Have you heard of that one before?

Slack is super cool. Again, it's free. If you go to any of my iPads, phones, if you go to any of them, you'll see that Nozbe and Slack are side-by-side at all times on all my stuff. Slack is basically super cool for project management. I'll create, they call them channels, but I'll create a page, right? Let's say I'm going to do a house on

417 Augusta. That's a house I've got going on right now. I'll create a page just for 417 Augusta.

Then I will invite via email whoever I want to be included on this house, which is basically going to be my contractors, like my project managers, if I have a superintendent, my electrician, my EMPs, whoever it is that I'm going to be working with; even my real estate agents, mortgage people. Anything that is going to be working in this house, I invite all those. They all join. Once you have that channel, you can basically create subchannels. That means I'll have a folder for exterior, a folder for interior, roofing, all the different bedrooms. Whatever it may be, I'll create folders down the left-hand side which will always be there.

Then, I may invite certain people to join certain folders, where other people don't need to be involved in this folder at all. It allows me to keep it private where some people can't see it and then some people can. Let's say I'm doing the kitchen. When I go in the folder for kitchen, I'll put everything that has to be done inside of this folder for the kitchen and whoever is involved with it will always get notification that hey, here's what's going on inside the kitchen, here's who it's assigned to. Basically, when they respond, they don't email me, they don't text me.

Their response goes right back in the Slack. It's a communication form, as well. If I put out there, "Hey are the cabinets done today?" Say Jim's into the cabinetry, oh sorry, you're Jim, let's say Bob is into the cabinetry, "Bob are the cabinets done today?" He can respond right back in it and it gives me the date and time. If I ever find a contractor, which I know you've dealt with this before, contractors not always telling the truth on something is done/not done, whatever, I can go back to this file and it says hey, on Tuesday at 4:03 PM, you write, "The cabinetry is done."

Again, when you're doing these cabinets, the guy, he says that he was done Tuesday at 4:03 PM; he shot me a message on Slack that he was done, I showed the house at 11:00 on Wednesday at 11:00 AM and the upper cabinets aren't even done. I can to go back to my app right from my phone and it basically allows me to keep the contractors on check and then it allows me to get room-by-room so all my work is done. It's a great, great productivity app if you're doing the buy, fix and sales. You could use it for other stuff, but I use it a lot for that. That's called Slack.

The 2 productivity apps, I'm sorry, Jim, I gave you a lot more than you asked for, but 2 productivity apps, #1 is Nozbe, that's my command center for what I've got to get done today and then #2 is going to be Slack; that's more of a project management house flipping app that I use. Both are free. Both are absolutely great.

Yes, S-L-A-C-K. Slack just recently became a billion dollar company just recently. It was created by the founder of Flicker. The founder of Flicker built Slack. I use EverNote a lot. I used to use EverNote a lot. It was my command center, but with these new apps that are coming out and all of these will integrate. Slack will integrate with EverNote. Nozbe will integrate with EverNote. Sometimes I'll still use EverNote, but EverNote became a ginormous storage center for me of all my different bigger projects, goals, and all kinds of stuff like that that I save stuff in.

As far as productivity, sometimes EverNote is overwhelming because it does so much, it will do so much for you, to keep it simple, Nozbe is freaking awesome and then Slack is another that's just absolutely great that I use. Slack you can't use for your day-to-day operation, but it's good for flips.

Jim: I know, but just exactly for that, though. A lot of people listening are going to be doing flips. To keep a specific property, that's awesome. I've been doing this 7 years. I've interviewed 25 of the top guys from around the country and that's the first time I've ever heard of that app.

Andrew: The biggest thing is I'm a real investor, so a lot of times you hear from different people, but I'm out there every single day trying to figure out what's working, what's not working, what schemes are working, what material is working and those are 2 apps, man, that are really, really good and useful. Of course, the inbound marketing strategy, I told you 99% of anybody out there is not using it.

There's a great book that after everybody has read this book that you're putting out, if they want to learn about the inbound marketing, there's a book called "Blue Ocean Strategy."

I don't even know who wrote it. I read it a couple years ago. Eddie gave it to me. It's called "Blue Ocean Strategy" and it's just a great understanding marketing. Basically, in a nutshell, sharks always go to the red oceans, meaning that's where the blood is at. There's that 1 house pre foreclosure and there's the blood and boom, all these sharks are headed over there and it creates this red ocean.

The ones that are really successful focus on the blue ocean in which there's not sharks there because you're there before anybody else gets there, so you're there during the calm waters called blue ocean strategy. It's just a marketing book that's absolutely great if you want to learn. It doesn't really talk about inbound/outbound, but the concept of it is blue ocean marketing. It's a cool little book.

For more information on Andrew and his company visit:

www.AndrewCordle.com

Jeff Watson

Jeff has been a lawyer since 1991 and a landlord and real estate investor since 1994. His experience includes rehabbing, creative buying and long-term holding of numerous rental properties and apartments, short sales, and doing private lending and transactions inside self-directed retirement accounts.

Jeff is a frequent popular guest speaker and teacher on stages all across the country as well as on webinars. He is recognized throughout the real estate investing world as an innovator on wealth building and self-directed retirement transactions. As an attorney, he currently represents established investors in commercial and residential matters, particularly when they are investing using their self-directed retirement accounts.

Jeff is the co-creator of the option contract method that dramatically changed the short-sale process and the transparency of it when people were selling the transactions back-to-back for quick turns.

Jeff's Answer:

I would learn both how to do and explain wrap mortgages to other investors so they would want me to wrap their loans to rehabbers. I would also do "Lonnie deals" on mobile homes. Those are two types of transactions where I can take a little bit of money, say $1000, and leverage it to triple my investment in a year's time.

I'd be doing $1,000, $1,500, or $2,000 dollar deals. If that was all the capital I had, then I'd be doing wrap mortgages where I wrap my $1,000-$2,000 around someone else's $25,000 or $125,000 or $200,000 to put into a third person's hands to get a rehab or cash-flow deal done. That's what I'd be doing.

Jim: The wrap mortgage, maybe you can explain that in a little more detail, because that might be a new term to some people.

Jeff: Sure, let me give you a high-level overview. A wrap mortgage is when I'm going to take my little bit of money and use it to encompass or encase a larger sum of money that then gets lent to an end borrower. The end borrower makes a payment back to me. From the payment I receive, I then make a payment to the person who put 98% or 99% of the money into the transaction.

If I negotiate things right, I get an override on their money as well as my money. That's what gives me a phenomenal rate of return. If I don't do it as a wrap, then I'll do it as what I call a "synergistic second," a term I have trademarked. My second feeds off somebody else's first. I can then do some fantastic deals and see very high rates of return when I do these. I currently seek to do about one of these a month. I see a rate of return above 100% annualized on each deal.

Jim: Wow. That is impressive. 150% return and ... wow. It sounds like a complex thing to explain though so you really need to understand that. I guess that's why learning how to explain that is how you started that, and that's why because it seemed like a very complex thing to explain.

Jeff: It is a complex thing to explain. I've heard other people talk about it for years, and it never made any sense to me until I sat down and said, "Listen, there's got to be a better way to put my money to work." With what I learned from some really smart people and what I taught myself, I figured this thing out and created the synergistic second model.

If you ask me what I would do first, my answer is that I would learn the business. I would learn how to become a disciplined investor by finding a good strategy and sticking with it. For me, a good strategy is something that is low risk, high return. It should be something that is simple for me to do and understand, but something that nobody else really understands. That's where I'm going to make my margin of profit. That's the niche where I'm going to get rich.

Jim: Obviously that makes a lot of sense, and sticking with one thing and learning it, of course, makes a lot of sense. A lot of people do get into this business and get the shiny object syndrome. They go from one thing to another to another, because the thing they're doing, they haven't given it enough time or learned the process enough to make it work. All these different ways to invest in real-estate, they all work. They've been working for years.

You have to learn how to do it and really hone your craft in order to make it profitable to you. I think that people jump from thing to thing too quickly because they're not making money fast enough and they're probably going into the wrong niche, I would think, and not learning enough about it, but you mentioned.

Jeff: Like you said, I think shiny object syndrome is really what it is. To me, it's all about the fundamentals. I've learned a lot after doing this for twenty years. If I could have known twenty years ago what I'm saying to you now, I hope I'd have been smart enough back then to listen to me.

I'm reminded of the movie in which Ernest Borgnine plays the role of legendary football coach Vince Lombardi. He stands up in front of the Super Bowl champion Green Bay Packers, holds up an oblong object, and says, "Gentlemen, this is a football." What he was doing was going back to the very basics.

Often we're in such a hurry to get to the shiny that we run right over the basics. We forget them, we ignore them, and then we get into all sorts of deep trouble. There are some basic fundamentals that I would love to share with you.

The first thing I would tell you is to never, ever, ever borrow money from a bank. If I could go back and eliminate every bank loan that I've ever used, my life would be so much better.

Yes, I've made money on some deals, but the stress, hassle and aggravation of dealing with bank loans has made me regret it. Never again will I borrow money from a bank.

The second thing is that I would learn the self-directed IRA business at the inception of my investing business, because those are the people with money that I want to talk to. It's their money that I want to put to work with my money and go do deals.

Jim: It's actually with that you can turn almost anybody you know into a private lender, right?

Jeff: Exactly and I'm going to tell you Jim, one of my favorite cities to be doing the deals that I've just described to you is where you live in Chicago. I love investing in Chicago right now.

Jim: I enjoy it too, but it's not common. Not a lot of people do not tell me they like it here. The prices are little higher in some cases, but the south side you can get some good stuff for cheap.

Jeff: I'm going to tell you this; I love Chicago for one simple reason ... cash flow. I love the cash flow that comes off the properties that I lend on. The cash flow, see that's two words that every real-estate investor needs to write down everywhere they look. Its cash flow, you don't pay your bills with equity. You don't eat an equity sandwich. You pay your bills; you buy lunch with cash flow.

Jim: The rents here are good. I'm sure that's why you're getting what you're getting at.

Jeff: That's exactly where I'm going with this. It's a place where people want to live, and those who can afford it will pay to live here. That's why cash flow matters to me. Cash flow, cash flow, cash flow.

I would also tell you to do everything you can to minimize and eliminate risk. Your question asked me what I would do first if I had to start over not having much money. I would say to myself, "I've got little money to invest, and I want to make sure I have little or no risk." If a deal blows up and the most I've got at risk is $1,000 or $2,000, I can live to fight another day.

Never, ever, ever go all-in on one deal. I've been there and lived to tell the story about it, but I'll tell you what, it was a brutal, ugly time.

Jim: That's part of the basis for this book that people are reading right now, is to learn from these very experienced investors mistakes, and yeah what to avoid and how to avoid it; ways to invest with little to no risk. If you can figure that out early and master it you'll be golden in this business.

Jeff: Yes, and now I'm going to share with you a couple of things that are really radical. I warned you I was going to say this.

Those people who buy real estate, fix it up, and re-sell it are not investors. They are just very good business people. Houses are their inventory. They're just like car salesmen. They're dealers. Investing is a thinking-person's business; it is not a running-person's business.

You have to become disciplined. You have to find a good strategy and stick with it. Investing is what you do with the money left over from your paycheck, from your commission as a real estate agent, from your brokerage money, or from whatever job or career you're doing. Investing is what you do with the excess. You have to learn how to live on less than you're making, invest that difference, and let it grow. That's how you really get rich in this business.

There's tremendous risk there. Jim, the amount of risk is astronomical. We just don't see it. The fact that I've been doing this business now for twenty years is a testament to two things: God's grace and getting good advice and good training over ten years ago before this whole thing blew up. When you're in business and one day, you have a net worth of over a million dollars, and then a year later, you have negative equity over every one of your properties, that's a really tough time to live through.

Jim: Through no fault of your own ... no obviously it was your fault for putting yourself in that position, but owning that much when the market can change and do that to you, obviously that's opening yourself up to risk that you don't have to do.

Jeff: Correct, but you're also opening yourself up for those kinds of risks that you can't control. I need to look at it and say, "Okay, from now on, I'm going to play with deals where if something goes wrong, what I lose is not going to break me."

Secondly, I'm going to be looking for stuff with huge up sides. I love obscene profits, particularly in a self-directed retirement account. A lot of the deals that I'm doing where I'm putting in $1000, I'm doing them with self-directed retirement accounts. I'm making a triple-digit rate of return, and I don't pay taxes on that profit.

Going back to what strategy I would focus on, I would learn how to do wraps inside and outside of my IRA or 401k, and I would learn how to do "Lonnie deals," that is, I would learn how to buy mobile homes cheaply and resell them on terms.

Going back to this what's the strategy? The strategy I would be is learn how to do wraps with my IRA or 401k and outside of my IRA, learn how to do Lonnie deals, learn how to buy mobile homes cheap and resell them on terms.

Jim: Can you explain a Lonnie deal real quick?

Jeff: Sure, a "Lonnie deal" is named after the late Lonnie Scruggs, a fantastic, classy gentleman from the Virginia Beach, Virginia area. I had the privilege of actually having dinner with him once or twice. Lonnie was the guy who came up with the strategy of, "I'm going to buy a mobile home from a guy that needs to sell it. I'm going to pay cash for it, and I'm going to get it at a good price. Then I'm going to turn around and sell that same mobile home, without much, if any, clean up, fix up or repair, and I'm going to sell it on terms."

I'll give you an example of one I just did in the last three weeks. I bought this beat-up old mobile home for $1,000. I turned around and sold it on terms for $300 dollars down and $120 dollars a month for the next twenty-four months. I will have turned $1,000 into over $3,000 in twenty-four months. I've got a two-year clock, and in two years' time, I will triple my money.

Jim: You've got to live in an area that has a lot of trailers I would imagine.

Jeff: There are a lot of mobile home parks in my area, and I look at them and say, "Where can people afford to live because I'm in the business of providing safe and affordable housing?" If I'm in the business of providing safe and affordable housing, a good quality mobile home deal is a great place to be.

I'm also in the business of providing decent, affordable financing by taking somebody with money they don't know what to do with and connecting them with someone who needs money but is not sure where to get it. If I can connect those people and put my money into the deal in the form of a wrap or a synergistic second, then I'm in the game. Those are my two strategies.

Jim: Well that is not what I expected to hear, so I'm glad we did this interview because that's not what I expected to hear from you and that's very interesting. Look at how little money is in those deals and how much you're returning; you're tripling your money on these very small investments. Anybody could do that if they learned how to do it.

Jeff: That's my point. I wish somebody would have walked up to me twenty-some years ago, smacked me upside the head, and said, "Hey, stupid, you want to get rich? It's going to take time, it's going to take some effort, it's going to take some study, it's going to take some networking, and it's going to take a little bit of brainpower. You're going to have to develop an elevator speech, you're going to have to go out and network, network, network, and guess what? You'll do it. And by the way, don't ever walk on carpet in a bank and borrow money, and don't ever personally sign a promissory note, and you'll be a whole lot better off. You'll sleep better at night, you'll have more money to show for it, and your life will be less complicated."

Jim: We could all use that, and then I think ... and you mentioned something about This is not ... With the realize from reading this, there's about 28 guys that they'll be able to read their interviews here, and what they'll realize, all of them, that this is not a get rich quick.

Is there ways to make money fast in real-estate? Sure, of course there is. There are some wholesale opportunities where you can make money quickly, but the guys who make this long-term, it's just that. They've set up a long-term business plan that works over and over and over again, and they make crazy, millions of dollars, most of the guys who are in here, or all of them, quite frankly. Every single one you see that set up a business, something to create long-term wealth, it's not a get-rich quick scheme because that's not what this game's all about.

Jeff: It's not. For me, the final component of this picture is that I am a landlord. Do I hate being a landlord? No. Am I proud that I'm a landlord? Yes. But here's my challenge…none of my five kids wants to become a landlord. How can I mold and reshape and reposition my real estate businesses into something that my kids will want me to train them in and will want to take over from me in another twenty years? What will they want to step into in their 30's saying, "Hey, Dad. Let me help you with this now."

It's not going to be chasing down rents, and it's not going to be dealing with tenants and toilets and turnover and all that other stuff. It's going to be handling paper. It's going to be cash flow and income streams. That's what they'll be interested in. So if I have to start over from scratch, and I have very little money to work with, I'm going to get educated, and I'm going to focus on an area that when I build it, the next generation is going to want to take the baton from me when I hit the exchange zone.

Jim: Well that's awesome. That's obviously very powerful information for someone that's new in the business to have. Again I'm going back to how little investment they would take up front. They can be out of an IRA, your own IRA for that matter or somebody else's.

Everybody's got an IRA and so you could turn anybody's retirement account into some sort of ... and figure out a way to pull money out of it, or even your own for that matter. You'd be tripling your money into your IRA with tax free at that.

Jeff: Correct, and I'm going to tell you that the number one account I work with right now is not my own IRA. It is my mom's IRA. Why? Because my mom is over 59 ½ years old, and my mom has had that account open for more than five years, so I want to grow my mom's IRA for two reasons. First, so she can have the benefit from it, and secondly, someday I will eventually inherit it.

Jeff's Productivity Tip:

It is eat right, sleep enough, and exercise every day. A fourth component is to feed my mind good things daily. Read a chapter out of the Book of Proverbs from the Old Testament every day. Get a hold of good material and read it. Consume it, devour it, put it into your mind as to how you think about life and business.

Get your hands on stuff like The Millionaire Mind by Thomas J. Stanley, Ph.D., or stuff by Zig Ziglar. Yes, he's passed away, but his stuff is gold. Get your hands on that. Feed your mind. Feed your mind, feed your body, take care of them both, and they'll take care of you.

Jim: Back to the basics. Can't get more basic, eat right, sleep enough, work out, and again put good stuff in your mind.

Jeff: Yeah, and I'll nudge it a little bit further. Set your alarm clock to go off before the sun comes up. Wake up early. Get up and get going before everybody else so that everybody else around you is reacting to you, and you're not responding and reacting to them. You're the leader, you're setting the trend. Your email went out first, you've cleaned up all the paperwork and stuff you need to deal with before the phone starts blowing up at 9:00 in the morning.

Jim: Yeah I once read an article that says the majority of successful/wealthy people in the world get up three hours before they have to leave the house. The average person that's struggling gets up an hour before they have to leave the house. You might be able to take something away from that, right?

Because obviously like you said, you're leading the charge, you're getting your day started. By the time you've got to go you've been up for three hours, you've worked out, you've eaten right, you've read something, and you're ready to roll.

People who are getting up an hour before, they're hardly even awake when they get to work or walk out the door. There was a part of the article; it was a great article I read. I think it was in INC Magazine ... it was I, but it just goes along with what you're saying here.

Jeff: I found back as an associate at a law firm grinding it out at 70 hours a week, I found that my most productive time was from 6:30 in the morning to 9:00.

Jim: Nobody else was there?

Jeff: Nobody else was there and I could clearly focus. My body was rested, my mind was clear, I didn't have a day's worth of interruptions and chaos and thoughts running into my brain. From 6:30 in the morning to 9:00 am, I got more stuff done than I got done from 9:00 to 5:00.

Jim: That's awesome; that's powerful stuff. It's not easy to do, it's a habit you've got to pick up; get up early, get your day started, but yeah, there's no question about it that it's powerful stuff, back to the basics.

Jeff: Well remember it goes back to this... You're right, you're so true with back to the basics. Think about it once again, I told you ... Vince Lombardi standing in front of the Green Bay Packers, "Gentlemen, this is a football."

Jeff: Talking about basic fundamental concepts.

Jim: That's a great way to put it in perspective. Even when you said that to me, I've heard that before, I've heard it a hundred times, that speech. People bring it up all the time, but just the way you explained it with just putting this in perspective, I thought about "Man, that's powerful stuff," to bring it all the way back to, "Hey, here's professional football players,. This is a football."

Just like it puts it all in perspective, brings it all back to what's important and why we're all here and what this thing is, and just that's why he's one of the greatest.

Jeff: Slow and steady wins the race. Slow and steady wins the race. I don't care how many times I read the story of The Tortoise and the Hair to my kids, every time the tortoise wins. While I learned that a multi-billionaire takes the time out of his schedule to make sure that his grandkids hear him read that story on a regular basis, I went, "Whoa, if a guy who's started with nothing and now is a multi-billionaire is doing that for his kids and his grandkids, don't you think I should be doing it as well?"

Slow and steady wins the race. Avoid the shiny objects. Don't be like the rabbit; the rabbit chased all the shiny objects.

For more information on Jeff you can visit:

http://www.watsoninvested.com/

John Cochran

John is founder of systemsaturday.com. This guy is also known as a king of systems. He has a multimillion-dollar real estate investor from Dayton, Ohio, with a very unlikely success story. He, like many real estate investors, John's early attempts at real estate were less than fruitful. He started out as a rehabber, bounced around from strategy to strategy for eight years, working everything from short sale to tax liens, like many of us do, all these different acquisition strategies, we figure out which one's the best and go from one to another.

After nearly a decade of backbreaking work, long hours, irregular income, which I'm sure most of you listening can appreciate, if you've ever been a real estate investor, John had nothing to show for his labors but a few rent-to-owns and nearly 600,000 in debt. Since then, John has created over 1,200 video systems, earning him the title the King of Systems, and things have never been the same.

When John applies his passion for systems to purchasing HUD foreclosures, it was only a matter of time before he cracked the code, discovering how HUDs computerized system, how it worked, and how to use it to his advantage. After using these systems to great personal success, John combined these systems into a comprehensive course on buying and selling HUD foreclosures, called HUD wholesaling, which I'm sure he'll talk a little bit about.

John now lives his dream of financial freedom, is the CEO of Buyers on Fire, Homebackers Realty, and Systems Saturday, but his primary passion is investing in others, so he has staffers dedicated himself to helping serious real estate investors with the tools to teaching, to replicate the systems of success without suffering the years of failure and debt like he went through.

John's Answer:

This is actually a very, very easy question for me and the reason that is because I had to do it from scratch. Just like what you had just said and my background and whatnot, basically what happened with me was I started investing into real estate and then I got my clock cleaned, and basically by getting my clock cleaned, I literally went into a lot of debt and then I ended up getting out of all of that debt, never filed for bankruptcy, foreclosure or anything like that, made my first $1 million when I was 26 years old, and then I got my clock cleaned again after that.

Based upon that happening to me, I had to start from scratch because I had no money, I had all this experience but I had no money. What I did basically to get totally debt-free and to build up to a multimillion-dollar real estate investor, a speaker, trainer, and all that stuff that I do now, is there's two things that I did. I was very, very high with buyers. Everybody and every book that you read and everybody will flat out tell you seller, seller, seller, sellers. It's exactly what you need to do, you need to go after the sellers.

Without a seller, you're never going to be able to buy a property, this and that.

They're absolutely right, but if you go and look at ... If you're totally broke and you have to go out and bring in motivated sellers, I don't care what anybody says, you're going to have to have some sort of money involved with it, whether it's a bandit sign, whether it's a billboard, whether it's something. You're going to have to have some type of direct mail, something. You're going to have to have money involved somehow and I didn't have that luxury at all, so I knew sellers was out. I just could not work with sellers because I didn't have any cash.

I knew that the fastest route to a paycheck would be if I was going to need money right, right now, which I did was I need to control all the buyers because if I had all the buyers, the sellers would naturally come to me. I looked at the acquisition of a seller and I said, "Okay, so if I'm going to spend $80 for a good seller or over $100 for a good seller lead that I don't have, I can't do that, but if I could go up and set up some type of website or something like that and attract buyers to it, I could get way more buyers into my pipeline than I would ever even have sellers."

The truth of it is, is that it motivated sellers, they're really not going to websites and filling out forms and all that stuff. That's really not what the motivated sellers that you're actually buying properties are doing. They're hiding and you got to go and reach them. What I did was I went and I built this big massive buyers list, I created a website for free, and I literally was giving away a free list of homes for buyers to search.

Now, in order for all of these buyers to search for all these homes for free onto my website, they would have to give all their contact information, their first name, email, and their phone number, so that I could actually call them. What I ended up doing was driving all these buyers to this site and then getting all of these hundreds and even thousands of buyers into my system, calling all of these buyers, and then just literally finding out the buyers who are motivated, the buyers who have money, the buyers that can buy now, and then I would just go and match them up with sellers on Craigslist or on somewhere.

Most of them were on Craigslist and by doing that, the first month that I did that, I ended up making 17,000 bucks just by going ahead and changing that strategy by everybody saying that you got to go sellers. I didn't have any money for sellers. I had to go after the buyers, they were totally free, you can go find buyers off of Craigslist, build your buyers list, just advertise that you're going to go out and you got this free list of homes in all these different areas, put all those ads on Craigslist, you're going to build your buyers list straight from that, and then you just go and match them up with sellers on Craigslist, and that's exactly how I made, started making it was with buyers.

Now, in turn with that is that since I ended up controlling all the buyers, now what I ended up doing was another free approach, because now I needed to go and find some sellers. Okay? What I ended up doing was I started by going to hudhomestore.com and started looking at all those HUD foreclosures. I was looking at all these HUD foreclosures and I knew that I was bidding against a computer. Okay? I knew that I was bidding against a computer and

I was also smart enough even being a hillbilly in Ohio, I was smart enough to know that if that computer is, if I'm bidding against a computer, I had to know that that when I submit an offer to that computer, it has to tell me yes or no, and it has to have prewritten guidelines in it. It has to. If it's the one doing it, it's got something programmed into it. I was smart enough to know that.

Then what ended up happening was I ended up buying a property for it was a property that was up on the market for 6,000 bucks, and I ended up buying it for 1,250 bucks, I got a realtor commission for 1,250. Bottom line, I ended up having at the end of the day, I ended up buying that property for 18 bucks. On that site, what you can do, it's all free properties, you don't have to market for any of these properties, and now that I controlled all the buyers, now I went to all this free different marketing on HUD, then I learned their bidding system, I learned exactly what made them tick, what would make them give me acceptances, what would make them give me counters, what were they accepting, what was the percentages, and all this stuff, so I ended up creating a spreadsheet out of it and I automated the entire process to where I started marketing or I started bidding on every single property that HUD had, every single day in my area because what I was doing once I was getting those acceptances, HUD does not have a deed restriction on any of their properties, so all I had to do was go and match all those buyers that I had up with those sellers that I got for free on HUD, because I figured out what their computer would take on every single property, and then I just matched those two up and then that's when I really started making a lot of money.

Jim: Wow. That is impressive. All that for free, too. Right?

John: I had to. I had zero money. I had zero cash. I did all of that for free.

Jim: You said you set up a website for free, and when you're driving traffic, that was all free, you just did with via Craigslist or what was the best way to go about doing that? You're obviously marketing for buyers at that point, right? You're not marketing for sellers, but it was still very cost-effective, right?

John: Yeah, so what I did was I ended up getting a free search onto our site, so I ended up getting a free search onto my website, created a website that looked pretty bad, but I was even marketing rent to own because I knew that rent to own buyers, they had down payment money. I knew that, so I was marketing rent to own, and then what I ended up doing was I was looking at all the different cities in our area and just say there are 12 different cities that I was working in my area. What I would do is I would create five different ads on Craigslist for 12 of those cities. Okay.

I'd have 60 ads on Craigslist every single day, so I do five ads for one of those cities every single day. I was blasting out if it was, I would do search all, bank-owned properties in Orlando, Florida. Search all bank-owned properties in Dayton, Ohio. Search all, 100 bank-owned properties in whatever. I was finding, I was building my cache database right there is exactly what I was doing.

That's how I lured them in was I had all of those ads out there so whenever they go to go and search for all those different bank-owned properties in one of those cities, they obviously are dropped to a page that is going to capture information, which will allow them to search those lists of homes in those cities.

Jim: Yeah, wow. You basically reverse engineered the whole process, right? You started with the end in mind marketing for the buyers who were going to buy it, then you went and found the sellers afterwards, which is usually what a lot of people do is the opposite, right? They find a seller when they get in the business and they

	go scramble to hope to find a buyer they didn't have already.
John:	That's exactly it.
Jim:	You would usually need to in what, five or seven days tops, you have to find one if you don't have in place and you're SOL, you got to let the property go and potentially lose a deposit.
John:	Yep.
Jim:	Wow. That's awesome. This is a wholesale strategy, essentially, right? You were just wholesaling HUD homes, which obviously is the name of your course, too, is HUD wholesaling, right?
John:	You bet. That's all it was, it's a wholesaling strategy of how the hell you're going to control all the buyers and then just go hook them up with homes. When people actually go through our course now, most of them, they end up making their first profit check in 30 days, which is exactly what I had to do, and everything that you do is free. It's something that I had to do to keep my head above water and then I was just

able to grow it and scale it and that's why they call me the King of Systems.

John's Productivity Tip:

1,000% what I stayed dedicated to from the very, very start and how you introduced me was I've created over 1,200 video systems. Every single Friday, every single Friday it's literally like clockwork. You cannot find me on Fridays. You cannot basically talk to me on Fridays. Nobody can really do any of that because all I do on Fridays is I look at all my systems, and that's how I perfected HUD, that's how I perfected all the buyers and everything. All I'm doing is I'm going through and I'm shooting about 10 video systems a day on Fridays and I'm very, very consistent with that.

What I do is every single ... I just have a sheet of paper with me. Believe it or not, I know every single system that I've done out of all those 1,200, I know every single one that I've done, I know everything that I haven't done. What I do and how I outsource is that I've got a sheet of paper with me every single day and when I do something, maybe it's just sending out an email or maybe it's putting a bid in on a HUD home or whatever it might be. If I did something that I don't have a system on already, I write it down on that piece of paper and then come that Friday, what I'll do is I will do systems, I will redo those systems on every single one of those things that I didn't have systems on, and then I will literally store it into a membership site for my team and then basically I outsource all those things so that we continue to grow. That's exactly what I do, I'm very, very consistent with that.

Jim: You're hardcore timeblocking Fridays.

John: Yeah, nobody can get a hold of me on Fridays. It's virtually impossible. I typically work from home or I work from my house, and I do that, I'm very consistent with it, and that's how I time block, that's how I get the time to perfect my systems, that's the time that I look at all my numbers in my business, that's the time I see all of our processes, what can we do faster, what is not working well, and all that stuff, and it's worked very, very well for me and that's why I feel like I have a very well-oiled machine.

To check out more on John and his systems visit:

www.TheKingOfSystems.com

Gregg Cohen

Gregg is the owner and CEO of JWB Real Estate Capital and since 2006 these guys have acquired over 1,200 investment properties. They do turn-key cash flow, and they have everything under one roof, from acquisition to property management. They've got a staff of over 35 people. They have clients all over the U.S., and in 12 different countries.

In 2013, they were ranked as the number 23 fastest growing company in Florida, and they were the number 12 fastest growing company in Northeast Florida by Jacksonville Business Journal.

In addition, they were ranked the number 12 fastest growing company in 2012 by Inc. Magazine. So, Gregg, thank you for being here.

Gregg's Answer:

Well, you know, when I think about how we did start back in the day, we didn't really have any money. So, it's pretty easy for me to go back there and just think about the things that made us successful in the beginning, and the first year for us was pretty tough.

It was tough to actually sell property, and as I go back and I think about it, it was because we didn't really know what the criteria was of our buyers. We were so focused on getting out there and locking up a contract, but you know, not every contract that we locked up sold, and it was because we spent so much time focusing on what we should be buying the property for, and not enough time focusing on what we should be selling the property for.

So, I started to think about this, and I get this question a lot from newer investors out there, and they're saying how can I be successful, and when I think about it now, it's pretty simple. If you invest in the relationships with the people that are actually going to be buying your property, you're going to be much better off. You're going to save yourself a lot of time, and probably a lot of money from spending dollars on marketing out there to lock up a deal that may or may not sell.

So, the thing about it is you don't have to have that many great relationships with the buyers. If you invest time, find the 3 to 5 biggest buyers in your area, and go to their office. Just say, "Hey, I want to be the best wholesaler that I can to you. Can I understand exactly how you buy so that I don't waste your time, when I bring you a deal, you're going to say yes 75 to 100% of the time?"

They would be open to that. I can tell you that because we're one of the biggest buyers in Jacksonville, and we love that when folks say that to us. We invite them in for lunch in our office. We sit down with them because they can help us, and of course we can help them.

So, if I had to think about what I would do over again when I was just starting, I would focus more on building relationships with the biggest buyers in the area, and learn everything about them, and focus on how I can make them more successful, and in turn make myself more successful.

Jim: So, still taking a wholesale approach then would mean finding the guys, the rehabbers or the investors that are buying and holding cash flow properties. Those are the guys that you'd find a wholesale deal through essentially?

Gregg: Yeah. Exactly. I would focus on wholesaling because I think that's the best way to get started, and I would go ... and here's how I would find the biggest buyers. It's all public information. You can go on to your county Website, and you can look for the most recent deeds that have been recorded. That means that properties were purchased. You could download this list. We can do it on our county Website. I'm sure you can probably figure out a way to do it on your county Website, and you get a list of all the deeds that have been transacted lately.

Then, you'll organize them, and you see which ... What are the names that keep showing up over and over and over. If you see somebody that's buying 20 properties, or more, a month, that's a big buyer. You should probably talk to those folks and see what you can do to help them.

So, you don't need to spend any money to figure this stuff out. You just need to know where to look. You can probably find it on your county Website. If not, it's available on the Multiple Listing Service. If you're not a realtor, you can ask a friend who's a realtor to download the list of the most recent sales, and just look for the biggest names, and when you find those big names, invest some personal time.

This can be a relationship that can make you hundreds of thousands of dollars as a wholesaler, if you just treat it with respect, and focus on how you can make them more successful, and in turn make yourself more successful, and I think that's absolutely the best place to start, and not many people do that. You know what I mean?

The best marketing strategy that we did that didn't cost any money was good old fashioned door knocking, back in the day. I love the concept of door knocking when you're getting started. For two reasons.

Number one, you're going to pick up a few deals that way. It doesn't cost any money to go and knock on a door, but the other thing is that it is going to teach you about getting rejected, and teach you how to pick yourself up and move on to the next one, which is incredibly important, in this business and every business.

So, if you don't know what I mean by door knocking, it means finding a distressed seller, and that may be that they are in pre-foreclosure, that may be that there's just a house that needs repairs, it might be that you see a home that's vacant that's a sort of an eyesore in the neighborhood, and going knocking on all the neighbor's doors next door, and asking questions, but that's what we did back in the day.

We pounded the pavement. I got rejected a billion times, but you know what? I locked up 5, or 10, or 25 deals that way too, over the years, and I think it's just the best way to get started.

You've really got to test how much you want it. I think that's important for folks in the beginning, because you've got to want this business really

	bad. It's not going to go easy. It is simple in theory, but in application and in execution, it takes a lot of hard work. So, I like the old-fashioned door knocking.
Jim:	Yeah, pounding the pavement. I think it's actually ... It's on my wall. It's a quote from Robert Kiyosaki and it says "failure inspires winners. Failure defeats losers". So, like that stuff you said you're getting rejected, rejected, and now what, 7 years later you guys have done 1.200 properties, and you manage, what, 650 or something crazy like that?
Gregg:	Yeah, you know, but it's funny. Whether the problem is a problem I'm working on right now, solving something in our business, or if it was way back in the day, when we hadn't put a deal under contract back however many years ago, it all comes down to just figuring out a solution, and in order to figure out that solution, you've got to want it bad. It's so easy to make excuses.

So, you just build on the success of locking up your first deal, you figure out a way to do it, you get rejected, you get told no a million times, and then you do it, and then that turns into 10, and then that turns into 100, and so on and so forth.

So, it all comes down to the same principles, and that's why I love folks. I get out there, pound the pavement, know they're throwing themselves to the wolves in a sense, and knowing that it's going to be very difficult, but you build a lot of confidence in your abilities that way, and in your business model, which serves you over the years.

I just think there's way too many people in this business that just want it to come easy. It doesn't come easy for a very, very long time in my opinion.

Gregg's Productivity Tip:

My productivity ritual is that I end the day by writing out my to do list for the following day. It's great because I start the next day ready to roll. But the biggest benefit for me is that when I write out what I'm going to accomplish the next day, I usually end up figuring a lot of the stuff out the night before. It's just something about writing it out, it makes your mind start to work subconsciously and I'll start thinking of ideas right before bed, or in the shower, or brushing my teeth. I don't know why, but it works!

For more information on Gregg and his

turn key cash flow company

Visit: http://www.jwbrealestatecapital.com/

Justin Colby

Justin Colby is co-owner of Phoenix Wealth Builders. Now, Justin's team has flipped well over 300 properties and they're currently wholesaling you flipping around five deals a month. He has a top-selling book on Amazon and a podcast on iTunes that are both named, The Signs of Flipping. He's a nationally recognized educator and speaker and I'm honored to have him with me today.

Justin's Answer:

Well, it's a great question. First and foremost, I always tell all of my students and clientele that there's only two ways to bind the deal in this real estate economy and that is to network or market and so, we're talking about the fact that we have very little money to market then networking is going to be my number one choice.

Now, there's a lot of different ways to network but things that I would focus on strategically would obviously be your REIA meetings, which is your Real Estate Investment Associations in your city. If you don't have that then I would start going to title companies in realtors.

I remember when I first started, I had no money. I was literally sleeping on a couch, me and my business partner, Law Star Homes, we had no income and all we did all day was cold call realtors to set up coffee meetings. So, we would sit at Starbucks. We would order one coffee and we would talk and network with realtors. From that came different contractors. From contractors came different wholesale investors. From wholesale investors came different hard money sources and as the saying goes, it keeps on going, right?

And so, the snowball started to run downhill. Another source of networking which now in today's time is much greater than it was when I started is your social media network. One of the best ways to do that is become and be along to all of your real estate investing groups that are on Facebook and LinkedIn and start engaging with these individuals, you know, asking questions, promoting a deal that you're looking at. Maybe post a picture and ask a question of whether you like these countertops or not. Engage with the individuals on all these different real estate investing social media networks and then you are going to be able to start building a relationship with these people, right?

And that is a major component especially on Facebook and LinkedIn as well as the other components which would be like Twitter or other social media campaigns. So, if you are low on cash to spend on marketing then I'm going to say networking is your next best option. Now, that being said, if you have a very small amount of money to utilize, what I would do is go out and get a list of motivated sellers. There are several ways you can do that one of which would be from your title company which would be free.

There are other companies out there like ListSource.com that you can buy a list of motivated sellers very cheaply. I mean very cheaply like a thousand sellers for way less than a hundred backs, probably closer to 50 bucks for a thousand and you can belong to what's called a skip-tracing company like Intelius.com. Now, their monthly fee is 19.95 a month but you get to run on limited skip-tracing. So, you can put it in the person's name from the list that you got from your title company and find their phone number.

Now, it's probably about 70 to 75 percent effective. So, you're not going to be guaranteed to finding a phone number for each and every one of them, but because you found a list of motivated sell... you to call those people, leave a message saying something as simple as, "Hi. My name is Justin Colby with Phoenix Wealth Builders. We're a small local real estate investment company here in the area looking for another investment property in your neck of the woods. If you're interested in selling your home at all or finding out what the value of your home is, please give me a callback at..." in your phone number, OK?

And so you go in there and spend all your time by calling these sellers from your list whether it'd be from your title company or from a list provider. Now, that is a very inexpensive way to find these sellers. So again, you either have the money to market or you have to network. Either way, you're either going to spend money or you're going to spend time. So, in this scenario, you need to be spending your time networking with as many wholesalers, fix and flip investors, private money lenders, title companies, realtors, hard money lenders as you possibly can so that they will introduce you to the next person.

And eventually, if you do this long enough, you will start to gain some traction and if you do have a very small marketing budget, I encourage you to find a list of motivated sellers. I always am looking for people with equity, OK. I don't want to deal with short sales or areas. I'm looking for people with equity so, I can negotiate with them so that I can wholesale their property. To wrap it all up, I would start by wholesaling. I would not try to become a fix and flip investor with no capital.

I would start by wholesaling, get a couple of paychecks. I would celebrate those wins. I would do it again until we started raising some capital to start marketing and when I started marketing, I would start using direct mail, write letters explaining that I'm a local investor looking to buy your home and then it would go from there and as I continue to wholesale and collect those checks, I then could get into fix and flipping because I'm starting to make a good amount of money and starting to ramp up my business.

So, if I had to do it all over again with very little money, to conclude, I would start by wholesaling. I would be networking my butt of at REIA meetings, title companies, realtors, hard money lenders, you name it, I would be trying to network with them and then as I have a little bit of money, I would be buying a list from ListSource.com or going to my title company trying to find people with equity in the zip codes I like and skiptracing them. Meeting, going into Intelius.com and putting in their name and in return, I would be able to get their phone number. So, at that off… I would focus on wholesaling.

Jim: So, when you said like the equity list or motivated sellers with equity, is that like a free and clear or like an absentee owner? Like what kind of list would you focus on when you're looking for that initial list when you're going to buy like your first list, what do you think is a good one for something to start with?

Justin: Yeah, free and clear or high equity and an easy way to judge whether it's high equity is people that pretty much bought between 1950 and 1990 most likely have equity because it was before the extreme rise and before the extreme fall of our real estate economy. So, the likelihood of them having equity is pretty good.

Justin's Productivity Tip:

Yeah, well. And you know that I know there... A lot of people probably heard this before but every single morning I wake up, I throw my feet off my bed just to get my blood circulating. I literally throw them off. Otherwise, I could go right back to sleep and I start just giving thanks and I have just an attitude of gratitude and I start thanking God for everything that I've been given from friends, family, work down to my car to gas to any of it and it starts my day off on the right foot each and every day because I start my day out by being thankful and that is the one thing I can truly say has really helped with our success.

For more information on Justin and his company visit:

www.TheScienceofFlipping.com

or email them directly at info@thescienceofflipping.com

Tim Mai

Tim has done over 500 deals, but Tim has done 500 deals and where he came from prior is really the more impressive part than the 500 deals because that's impressive on its own but Tim was actually born in Communist Vietnam and he and his brother had to escape to get here on a boat, literally, and this guy's got a crazy story.

He came here when he was 11, didn't speak much English. He took to school. He took very well to school. He did well in school. He got out. After college, got a job as an IT consultant only to be laid off on a company-wide layoff through no fault of his own, so very frustrated of course at that point like anybody would be. This guy has worked hard through school, got laid off through no fault of his own. He found real estate investing, so he became a bird dog originally like a lot of people start in the real estate investing business, and now he's worked his way up to be one of the country's top real estate investors and he's done well over 500 properties.

Now he has a company called Prosperity Real Estate Group that's in Houston which is where he's been, and they focus on teaching people in live seminars, workshops, the real estate investing business. He's also an extremely sought after mentor. Guys are paying him upwards of 120,000 for business coaching, which when he takes their business from six figures to seven figures, obviously is a deal. It may seem like a lot to you initially, but 120,000 if he takes your business from 500 to a million, well, 120,000's pretty well worth that then. Tim has also pioneered using virtual assistants, or VA's as they're commonly known in our industry, or in any industry, for real estate investing, so he's gone on to have virtual assistants in virtually every aspect where he's almost completely out of his businesses.

Tim's Answer:

Right. Okay. There's a lot of ways I can answer that and it really obviously depends on your situation of whether you have more time, more resources, or not much time, not much resources, but I'm going to keep it simple and I'm just going to assume that your brand new to the business, you don't have much money, and maybe you don't even have much time because you're working a full-time job. I'll begin from there and one of the ways that we teach our students, and it's one of the easiest fastest ways for you to start doing deals is just simply by letting everyone in your contacts know you buy houses.

A lot of people make marketing very difficult. "I don't know anything about marketing." Marketing is nothing more than how many people know what you do. That's it. Your job is to get more people to know what you do. The first place to start is with your family, your friends, your cousins, your Facebook friends, wherever that you can let people know that "Hey, I'm getting into real estate investing and I'm looking to buy some houses. If you or someone that you know needs to sell a house quickly, please let me know."

By doing that simple thing, a lot of our students have gotten deals from their cousins, from their co-workers at work, and made money within days. For me, that wasn't the strategy I got my first deal with, however, that was a strategy that I got my second and third deal with after I bought that property. After I bought my first property, my second property was from the neighbor to the left of that house who is a real estate agent and she let me in on a listing that she just got and then the third house that I got was from the neighbor to the right of the first house that I bought.

Yeah, so from simply letting people know what I do, people just started to bring me deals, so tapping into your network is really, really important. My first private lender that funded my first deal was my sister because now she knows what I do, so while she didn't have a house to sell to me, she had money to lend to me for my first deal. It can go in so many different ways whether they become a seller to sell you their property or they can become your private lender or they could become your buyer to buy a property from you, so definitely start there.

As far as your exit strategy of what you're going to do with those properties, it's really up to you, but wholesaling is one of the easiest ways to get started and learn the business. Wholesaling is basically you get a property under contract, you find another buyer that will buy it, and you assign your contract to them, making your quick assignment fee and you're out of the deal, so there's no holding costs. There are no risks that are involved in that, so wholesaling would definitely be a strategy I'd recommend that you get started with.

Wholesaling is it's a really simple thing that I think anybody can do it. Most of us, if we look on our contact list, we would have I think at least a hundred people on our contact list. In my case, it's a couple thousand people, but just on my phone.

Email is a great way to do it. Just off of your phone contact list is another way. You can just text them. Your Facebook. If you tap into Facebook, I'm sure you have a few hundreds if not a few thousands of people there, so that's a great place to start, and then another really easy place to also start that's also free is Craigslist.

When I first got started, Craigslist didn't exist, so I had to use the local newspapers at that time, but the same strategy would apply. You have these for-sale-by-owners that try to sell the house on their own or even wholesalers that are listing their properties on Craigslist as well. The strategy I like to do with Craigslist is go after the older ads, so typically when a seller firsts list a house on Craigslist, they get a lot of people contacting them, so they're not that motivated, but 30 days down the line, if they haven't sold the house yet, there's a much higher motivation level there. I recommend that you find ads that are ... When you go on Craigslist and you do your search, go to the last page and then work your way back.

Craigslist, their rule is they'll run the ad for 45 days and after that, they take it off, so basically, you're working leads that are 45 days back. You'll start calling them and then another great source of leads on Craigslist that not a lot of people know about is for rent ads because when you have a house that's for rent, more than likely, it's a landlord that's selling it. It could be an intentional landlord, I call them. These are people who specialize in buying properties, fix it up, and rent them out. They're professional landlords, and there are also accidental landlords.

These are people who couldn't sell their house, whether it's their primary house, they bought another house, they upgrade, downgrade, and they couldn't sell the one that they used to live in, or it's an investor who got in and didn't know what the heck they were doing with landlording. They thought that was the way that they were going to become real estate millionaires, and now they got their share of the tenants and toilets headache and now they just want to get out of the business, so get out of landlording, and so they're trying to rent the house, but if they're trying to rent the house, guess what that means. It means the house is vacant. That means they're not making any money on it.

Here's a house that's vacant, they're not making any money on. They just want to get out in a lot of cases, so you contact them and say, "Hey, I notice that you have this house for rent and I was wondering if you're interested in selling it instead of just renting it?" If they say, "Yes," guess what. You've got yourself a really good lead, and if they say, "No," guess what that means. That means they're professional landlords and that they're looking for more properties to buy.

Jim: Now you have yourself a cash buyer potentially.

Tim: Exactly, so it's a great win-win. It doesn't cost you any money. It's just a little bit extra time to make these calls. You can call them, you can email them, and a lot of time, if they put their phone number, chances are it's a cellphone number because almost everybody uses that nowadays. You can text them as well. Texting typically gets you the highest response, more than email, more than phone calls, and so yeah, that's another great easy place for you to start.

I'm training my niece and my nephew and also his friend. My nephew's friend, he's now at an appointment right now to get a property under contract for, get this ... $5,000.

Jim: Where? In Houston?

Tim: In Houston, yeah. It's in a lower income area, but still, it's worth retail market, and it would be worth at least 70,000 bucks. Obviously, you don't always get lucky like that, but there are these type of deals and what I'm sharing with you guys right now is, and I'm using "you guys," Jim, because obviously there's an audience that's going to be listening to or reading this interview, so I want to make sure I include the audience here into this conversation.

That's what I've been having my niece and nephew and their friend doing is exactly what I'm teaching you to do is reach out to their contacts, reach out to the people on Facebook because these are college kids. They don't have any money. Putting money into marketing is out of the question for them at this point, so these are free marketing that you can do.

Another free marketing that you can also do that I literally just got a property under contract from them was they found a wholesaler that had a property that they were trying to wholesale and I do wholesaling. I do rehabbing. I do landlording, and so I'm always looking for all different types of deals, but they found this really good wholesale deal that I'm buying and so reaching out to other wholesalers in your area for deals is another great way, and then with you calling all these landlords, the ones that want to buy more rental properties, you find out from them what kind of criteria are they looking for so then you can then go to a wholesaler to have these deals and you get the property from the wholesaler and you sell it to that landlord, and voila, you've got yourself a deal and make some money, so reaching out to other wholesalers is another great free source of leads of deals as well.

They've already done all of the legwork of marketing, negotiating, putting that property under contract, determining the value of the property, determining the repair amount, so you're really short-cutting your entire process to just sell it to another landlord, mark up $3,000-$5,000, or even depending on how good the deal is, mark up even more than that to sell it to the landlord. Those are all free marketing that you can do to get deals very, very quickly. If you really focus and do this using the three strategies I share with you right now, you should be able to get your first deal within the first week of doing this business.

Jim: That's awesome. This is great information, all free. This is stuff that anybody could do. Right now, everybody's got Facebook, everybody's got contacts. At the very least, you can go out and find other wholesale, even if you don't know anybody, which everybody knows somebody.

You can go find wholesalers right now in your market on Craigslist or wherever. Call up bandit signs or whatever and you'll wholesale their properties for them. Do it double wholesale, and just to play on what you said there, it's basically a double wholesale. I have a student of mine that did a double wholesale deal where he was the second wholesaler and he made $20K. It wasn't even his deal. He did nothing. He went and found the guy and said, "Hey, could I sell that, too?" and so the wholesaler made his spread and my guy made his co-wholesale or double wholesale. It was like 20 grand on top of it, so that was great. Obviously, it's a great opportunity there, and they've already done all the work, like you said.

Tim: Yeah, exactly. I'll share with you a deal that I did that's crazier. You're talking about co-wholesaling or double wholesaling. How about a quadruple wholesaling?

Jim: What?

Tim: I got a deal on a contract for 50,000 and then I wholesale it for 85,000 to another wholesaler. Then he wholesales it to another wholesaler for

	100,000 and that wholesaler sold it wholesale to the end investor rehabber for $110,000.
Jim:	Really? Obviously, you got it for a great price at 50.
Tim:	Yeah, it was a fire damage deal, and I love deals that meet a lot of appearance that people run away from. I've made a lot of money with fire damage deal, with mold claim deals, deals where the insurance company had paid off the house, basically, and now the seller owns it free and clear. It gives me a lot of room to negotiate the prices down, so yeah, I got a really good deal on it and every single person in that transaction got a good deal.
Jim:	Yeah, really. It sounds like everybody made a lot of people happy. Hopefully the end rehabber made some money, too.
Tim:	Yeah, exactly.

Tim's Productivity Tip:

I'm going to answer that in two different ways and I'm going to relate back to share because the free marketing that I just shared with you is great to get you started, but if you want a real business that is consistent and is scalable, you can't stop there. One of the things I teach my students to do is that you have to reinvest your profit back into marketing and in my marketplace, 14% is the minimum amount that I want to reinvest back ... 14% of my profit is how much I want to reinvest back into marketing and so I recommend that you do the same. Different markets are different depending on how much it's costing you per deal, but somewhere between 14 to 20% is a good number.

If you want to be a rock star investor and you want to do a lot of deals every single month, every single year, so you can make a lot of money is that you've got to reinvest your profit back into your marketing. Direct mail is one of my favorite types of marketing. It's very scalable and it's very low cost per deal, so that's a marketing tip and a productivity tip because I don't just want you to do your first deal. I want you to make your first 100,000, make your first million dollars, and beyond.

The second productivity tip that I'm going to share with you, it's extremely simple, but at least 95%, if not 99% of people don't do this is putting things on your calendar. People use a calendar on and off. They especially put things on the calendar if it's birthdays, if it's holidays, but putting things on your calendar to follow up with a seller, putting things on your calendar to do your marketing that day, that time. Putting things on your calendar for everything that you do in your business, and really begin to utilize your calendar religiously because that's how you keep things in existence and it's real for you because when it's in your mind or when it's in a piece of paper somewhere, a lot of times you can't find it, you forget, but when you put things in your calendar, every single morning when you wake up, boom, you already know what you need to do for the day.

You're not like most investors just wondering, "I don't know what I'm going to do today. Oh, maybe I'll work on my website today. Oh, maybe I'll work on the postcard. Maybe I'll make this call." If it's on your calendar, it's like, "Wow, my day's already mapped out for me."

Jim: That's great. With all the online tools, Google calendar is free now. You have no excuse not to do it, and obviously, coming from a guy like you, just write it down so you see it in front of you. You have no excuse not to with all the free tools that are out there to make it easy for you.

Tim: Exactly, and the calendar, whether you use Google calendar or if you're non-techy and you use a normal paper calendar, it doesn't matter what calendar or what organizer. I'm trying to keep things very simple here because, of course, we can have a lot of productivity tools, but I want to keep things very simple, and the simplest things are the things that people forget, but it's extremely, extremely valuable and very effective and efficient, so yeah. Actually use your calendar more than just your vacations and your holidays and your birthdays.

Use it in your business and put down everything that you do, and then from there, as you get better at this, you want to look at how much is your time worth. I'm really big into automation and outsourcing and delegation. I can make a phone call and talk to a seller, but see, doing that kind of stuff is not going to get me paid $5000 an hour that I want to be paid, so there's plenty of people that I can pay them, like a virtual assistant, $3-$5 an hour or even an in-person $15, maybe $20, $30 an hour, or a really good person maybe even $50 an hour. It's still a lot cheaper than the $5000 an hour that I place on the value of my time.

Once you start making money, just like how you reinvest your money into your marketing is you reinvest your money to buy your time, so that way you focus on the part of your business that's going to make you the most money and you outsource the rest. If you want to make a million dollars a year or even a billion dollars a year, you got to look at what is your time worth and then from there, figure out who you need to put in place, what systems you need to put in place, so that way you can earn that kind of money that you want to earn.

For more information on Tim and his

company visit: www.DoDeals.com

MITCH STEPHEN

Mitch is a very successful real estate investors in Texas. He is author of the book MY LIFE & 1,000 HOUSES Failing Forward to Financial Freedom and MY LIFE & 1,000 HOUSES 200+ Ways to Find Bargain Properties. He specializes in the art of the owner financing deal and has done over 1,300 owner financing deals since 1996. Mitch also has a "Hard Money Loan" business where he lends money to other local investors, to the tune of about $6,000,000, in the San Antonio market where he's from. In addition to all that, Mitch also owns 16 boat and self-storage facilities over 1,100 doors! So, this guy is truly a rock star, and I'm honored to have him with us today.

Mitch's Answer:

All right, if I had to start over, I would find a place that had affordable housing, somewhere in the U.S.A., probably Texas, Georgia, Florida, Mississippi, Missouri, Alabama, Arkansas, any place that had affordable houses, not in the war zone. When I say, "Affordable" I mean houses I could buy and then retail for $120,000 or less. Once I decided on a place, I would move to that place, if I had to, and I would start buying properties with other people's money, OPM. I would start owner financing them for double what

I had borrowed. I would learn to master the art of owner financing. I like owner financing because in my opinion, it is the best strategy in the creative real estate arena.

I use to be a landlord. In my, book Failing Forward to Financial Freedom. I talk about the pro's and con's of being a landlord. I know there's a lot of people that have made millions of dollars using the buy and hold strategy. I'm not saying that being a landlord doesn't work, it's just not for me. WHY? ...because I don't like situations where I receive a payment, and then I don't really know if the money's mine or not. Let's face it, if one of a hundred things happens, I'm going to have to write a check because, as a landlord, I'm responsible for just about everything that can go wrong in a house. As a landlord, I'd get a payment in my hand, and the check would clear and I'd have the cash in the bank, and then a few days later the air conditioner breaks and apparently the money that was in my bank was not mine, it was the air conditioner man's. I ended up doing a heck of a job collecting money to give out to the roofer, and the plumber, and the air conditioning man, and the electrician, and the window replacement guy, and the carpet cleaner guy, but I wasn't getting to keep any of the money I was collecting. The money I was supposed to be making on paper was NOT hitting my bottom line!

So my book My Life & 1,000 Houses Failing Forward to Financial Freedom, depicts how I morph from being this very disgruntled landlord into a business that worked for me. I am now the bank!

When someone sends me a payment, it is a mortgage payment. If the toilet breaks, don't call me, I don't own the toilet, the owner owns the toilet. Just think of it like this Jim. When your toilet breaks, do you call your mortgage company and ask them to come out and fix it? No, You don't, do you?

In my early days, I had amassed 25 properties that had $300 spreads between what I owed and what I collected in rent. I had this plan, and I was supposed to have $7,500 profit coming in. At the end of the year, with the vacancies and the damages, and the non-pays, and all the other liabilities, I was losing money. I became very disgruntled.

I tried to sell those houses in conventional ways and it didn't work. I eventually hired the mentor to get me out of this rental mess and sell off my properties. I didn't want them anymore. My Mentor said, "Why don't you just owner finance them?" I'm thinking, "Ok, How do I do that?" He replies, "Take $3,000 down, on each of your 25 houses, and create a note the gets you the same exact spread, but this time you'll get to keep the spread." Overnight, I sold all 25 houses on terms. I got an average of $3,000 down payment each home. Suddenly, I had $75,000 cash in the bank! That was not a deposit, that was a down payment, and it was my money! When the payments came in, they stayed in my bank account and never left. Needless to say, I became a big fan of owner financing.

You see, to believe in owner financing, you have to believe in at least two things:

#1. You have to believe that someone paying $750 for rent would rather pay $750 to own. Do you believe that Jim?

Jim: YES!

#2. You have to believe that if that current occupant/payer dies, or otherwise quits making payments, there is a line of other renters that want to take his place? Do you believe that to be true Jim?

Jim: YES!

So let's say we've proven the rents are $750. Now, subtract $50 for insurance and I subtract $100 for property taxes. That leaves me with $600 that this person can afford to pay for principal and interest. If you use the terms 10.5% for 20 years, it means a renter in the area can afford to finance $60,000. I picked those terms Jim, because I've never owned a financial calculator in my life. I can look at $60,000 and know the P&I payment is going to very, very close to $600. I do calculations with my $1.98 calculator that I have to hold up to the sun to get started.

So, in this example, they can afford to finance $60,000. Then, as a general rule, we'd add 10% on for a down payment; $6,000. So the Owner Financed Value (OFV) is $66,000. Since we're not crossing over a threshold I may even decide to pad my price and move it up to $69,000. Since we don't need an appraisal, it's really just up to me and the buyer what the price is. This is a very important point: we don't need any appraisals or inspections. The buyer and the seller just have to agree.

The most import asset you have as a real estate investor is your ability to assess, quickly and accurately, the value of the property you are considering buying. If you know what you can sell something for, you know what you need to buy it for to make a profit. Finding the average rental comparisons can be very easy using apps and websites like Rent-O-Meter, Trulia, and Zillow. They are amazingly accurate. When you use these sites plus the Tax Assessor's site and your basic knowledge of what Insurance costs run per thousand$$$, you should be able to assess the OFV immediately; while sitting in front of a property in your car, on a laptop or smart phone, in about 5 minutes or less...for FREE!

Jim: Wow, that's great! Like you'd said, when you learned owner financing, you were doubling the amount that you had into it, is that what you were doing? So if you were into a house for $30,000 you were financing $66,000 with $6,000 down and financing the $60,000 @ 10.5% for 20 years or more? Is that how I understood that? You're making money to create a spread for yourself?

Mitch: Yes! Actually, I want a note for double what my investment is. This is a general rule. If I'm plus a few thousand it's still great deal. If I'm under, well, I can borrow more than $2,000 extra (in my left hand pocket...you'll see below)

Here we go! You guys got a pencil and paper? Write this down. I'm going to show you how to get paid up to 5 ways on one deal. This is how a typical deal starts out. I know the numbers are going to be low for some of you in parts of the country, but I've already explained, this strategy works best in areas where you can buy at bargain prices and then retail for $120,000 or less.

STEP ONE: I've done my homework. The comparable in the area were $750. I subtracted the $100 for Property taxes and $50 for home owner's Insurance and arrive at $600 for the P&I amount. I know the buyers in the area can afford to finance $60,000 so I add 10% on top to arrive at my OFV. I can owner Finance the subject property for at least $66,000.

STEP TWO: I contract to buy a house for $28,000 all in, closing costs, everything, $28,000 all in. I borrow $30,000. So, I just put $2,000 in my left hand pocket. And by the way, that $2,000 is tax deferred. You don't have to pay tax on borrowed money, until a major event happens. Major event meaning, the note gets paid off.

STEP THREE: Now we sell the property. I find a buyer who'll give me 10% down.... $6,000 down...and I finance the $60,000 balance at 10.5% for 20 years making their P&I payment $600/mo. By the time the buyer pays the $100 for property taxes and $50 for insurance they're right where they were when they were paying rent. It's that simple!

So, in this example, I've made $2,000 when I bought the house. I made $6,000 when I picked up the down payment when I sold the house. And I created a $400 spread between what I owe to my private lender and the P&I payment I collect;

$30,000 @ 8% interest only = $200/mo.

$60,000 @ 10.5% for 20yrs = $600/mo.

TOTAL CASH-FLOW = $400

In the recessions, when the house prices on the lesser parts of town were crashing, and 70% of the sales were in cash from investors, what do you think those prices and appraisals looked like Jim?

Jim: The values were falling!

Mitch: They values were down in the dumps, right? But what happens to the rents Jim, when you no one can buy a house?

Jim: Rents go up.

Mitch: YES! Rents are going up! So, if my owner Financed price is based on the rents, what is happening to the price of my owner financed homes?

Jim: The price of your owner financed homes are going up?

Mitch: YES! In the recession, while every other house was decreasing in their appraised value, my OFV was going up and up...right along with the rents?

Jim: That is impressive!

Mitch: Owner financed properties were going for more and more, while everyone else's prices are going down. The catch is, I didn't have to have an appraisal. I just had to make that renter happy that he was becoming an owner, instead of a renter.

So, if you boom in the bad times and you do pretty good in the good times, where is it left for me to fail? You would fail if;

A. You did not have integrity, because people who don't have integrity always fail.

B. If you don't learn your laws in your state and your county and how to deal with "Dodd-Frank" and some issues, but that's pretty simple. I won't get into all that, but basically there are people that you can hire. Their job is to keep you compliant. You just build it into your expenses.

Jim: What I gather from this is you would find a location that has affordable housing, where you could sell them for $120,000 or less. You'd learn how to do owner financing, which I just learned a ton about. That is just some of the most incredible information I've ever heard. It obviously is geographic in that you'd have to have that pricing, so you've got to find the location and then learn owner financing. I'd say to find a mentor that can teach you!

All of us, including myself, and I still spend a ton of money on education every year because I'll never know everything that I need to know. I started my real estate career up with a mentor and I will end it with a mentor. I will always have a mentor. So I take that to heart; I find somebody else to learn from every year. I'm always wanting to learn something new and I'm sure you do too.

Mitch: I just got back from my mastermind. I paid $20,000 a year to sit in a room with about 80 people, who have also paid $20,000. We all have substantial financial statements and we all deal in creative real estate in one fashion or another. Every single year, it pays me to go there. I make more than the $20,000 I spend per year. And mind you, that's just the $20,000 to be a member of the club. That doesn't count my airfare or my meals or my hotels or my rent car, it doesn't count any of that. I also believe there's always another level to go to.

There's so much great technology out there and it's hard to keep track of all the best practices. The first time I attended that mastermind group meeting, I saw people living in one state that does not offer much in the way of affordable housing and so they're buying houses in another state that does. Then it struck me, these entrepreneurs are actually accomplishing the goal that most of us are sitting in that room trying to do. They were creating a business that they work on and not in. They have purposely picked a different state, because they're going to have to be forced to manage it from above.

If you're in a place and you really can't move because your family ties are too strong, or you're emotionally attached to where you live, or whatever, that doesn't mean you can't go to an affordable state like Georgia or Ohio, or Alabama, and build a business there. You should be able to run this business from the phone and a computer from anywhere that has internet service...including a cruise ship or resort!

Jim: If you had to pick one place, and it could be San Antonio where you live, where would you pick in the market to do your type of real estate, with owner financing. Where would you, if you could choose the perfect honey hole of affordability?

Mitch: Georgia and Texas have the same laws and they have the fastest foreclosure laws on the planet. You can foreclose in less than 45 days. I would pick a place that had a non-judicial foreclosure and I would pick a state that is predominantly run by Republicans, or had a Republican governor because they're business friendly and they believe in less regulation. I think in all of our business, we could use fewer regulations. I like Georgia and Texas, but I also like Alabama and Ohio. I've had very successful students in these areas. Alabama has got some of the most affordable houses on the planet. I've got some students there. In some areas buying one of those houses is like buying a used car.

When you get into really affordable houses that you can buy with OPM for say, $15,000–$20,000–$25,000, $30,000...it's so much easier to find the private money! Tons of people have $25,000 in an IRA somewhere. It's way easier to find $25,000 than it is to find $300,000 like in New York or California.

I got really good with raising private money. So many people have those little chunks. In fact, I had to start lending money out to my local competitors because I couldn't buy enough houses fast enough. I was able to get private lenders in at a very low entry levels. I bought a house for $12,000 the other day, so I went to someone who only had $15,000 in their account. Well, they're out of money but now they're recommending me. It's funny how that works when you pay people on time without fail; they bring you more business! I have between $3,000,000 to $6,000,000 out in the streets of San Antonio, Tx on any given day.

Mitch's Productivity Tip:

People ask me all the time, "Mitch, how do you find so much affordable, non-recourse, private money." I tell them, "I ask for it!" I deliver my elevator pitch for raising private money to at least ONE person a day...even if it's a homeless man on the corner. I have to say it to at least one person a day; "I help people make above average rates of return on their idle money, limiting risk by using very valuable real estate as collateral. Would you like my card?" Raising private money is a muscle you learn to exercise–every day! When people say, "I just can't find any private money." I ask them, "When was the last time you asked for private money?" I'm not surprised when they can't even remember? Perhaps that's why they don't have private money…because they don't ask for it. You have to relentlessly ask this world for what you want. Relentlessly!

For more information on Mitch and owner financing deals visit:

www.1000houses.com/menu

Chris Urso

Chris started his real estate investing business back in 2007 and really all facets of real estate like when a lot of us get into the business. Four years ago he started focusing really on buying apartments. Through his real estate investment company, URS Capital Partners. URS Capital Partners, get this, controls over 50 million dollars' worth of apartments in the Midwest and the Southeast. He has raised over 18 million dollars in private money,

Chris is actively purchasing, re-positioning and raising private money for his deals. He doubled his business this year and he plans to do the same next year. In 2011, he created a coaching program called Elite Apartment Coaching with a mission to help private real estate investors play a bigger game and create true wealth through the power of apartments. In the last three years in his coaching program, his clients have purchased over 40 million dollars' worth of real estate in 10 states. That is just incredible. Very impressive stuff.

His apartment coaching program, Chris it was truly able to change the lives of his clients and guide them to their financial goals.

Chris's Answer:

Sure. I'm just going to touch on the first part of that. I bought my first property in 2001. From 2001 to 2007 my wife and I did a lot of residential deals, one to four family, close to 60 houses that we did. I think the biggest thing that I would do differently- I was 21 years old then. Even when I bought my first apartment deal four years ago, I was only 31. We didn't have a ton of money so I think this applies and a lot of people get intimidated first and foremost. I think the best advice I can give someone is play a bigger game from the onset.

For some people it might be a 20 unit deal versus a single family rental. Push yourself to do deals that are going to produce greater results. That's the one thing that I wish I would have done earlier on rather than tinkering around with the 40, 50 thousand dollar houses for so many years. I see the results that I'm getting from doing just two deals a year at a much bigger level are producing huge returns for myself, my business, and my family.

Even without money, if I was starting from scratch, I would pick a strategy and get hyper focused on that strategy and try to be the best at it and play the biggest game that I can at that particular strategy. I bounced around way too much in the beginning. From fix and flips to short sales, whole sales, rentals, lease options, seller financing. You name it, we tried it.

Starting out without a lot of money, get hyper focused. Become the expert on that niche because that's how you're going to create value around yourself and then the money will come when the deals come. You're going to become the first- the perceived expert in that space. I hope that makes sense. That make sense?

Marketing strategy that I would focus on? Once I found my niche and became an expert in that niche just through immersing yourself in a ton of education and training and finding the right people to model, I would master the private money marketing. I think when you figure that part of the business out and you become an expert in a specific niche, you marry those two worlds together and your growth is exponential then. It's really infinite at that point.

I would really focus on people then money. I know that's probably a little bit different than what some people are used to hearing, but for my business, it's not like I do a ton of direct mail and major marketing for the deals, it's really relationship driven with brokers but we've really perfected private money. That's always evolving- go ahead.

Jim: When you say with brokers ... Private money we all know is relational. Some of the people listening might not be aware of that, but it's all relationship driven right? When you say with brokers, is that guys bringing money into the deal? Is that how that works?

Chris: Brokers for the deal side. When I say marketing ... Marketing for money maybe is the better way to position this.

Focus your energies, once you get your system down for the real estate side, marketing for money is essential. You don't want to wait until you have deals to go find money. That's the machine that needs to be running side by side. You can get 100 deals in your pipeline if you're really great at marketing for deals and finding deals, that's great, but if you haven't told a single person about what you're doing, you're not going to get a red cent for those deals and you're going to miss opportunities.

I guess my point is, develop a way for you to consistently do something and market to those folks that have the ability to become investors and educate them. It's really education marketing at the end of the day for private money. Filling them in every step of the way on what you're doing, the areas that you're targeting, the types of real estate that you're targeting, hosting small webinars. I've done breakfast meetings, dinner meetings, and cocktail parties. I've marketed to my entire wedding list when I had to raise money for a deal in the past. My wife didn't love it. My wife didn't love it but we marketed and we put 65 people in a room.

Jim: Did it work?

Chris: Yeah, absolutely it did. We raised like half a million dollars that night.

It's really marketing for money is probably the strategy that I would have focused on earlier because that's going to fuel your growth. If you're willing to put the time in to become a real estate investor and a full time real estate investor, and you focus on marketing for dollars, you can just step on the gas and go as fast as you possibly can when that money's behind you.

Jim: I guess what they could pull away from what your wife didn't like but helped you guys raise a half million dollars is, you never know who you know who has money. It could be anybody. Your wedding list, obviously some people close to you, cousins, relatives, family, friends, friends of your parents, whoever. Anybody you know could become a potential private investor. It doesn't have to be some big rich guy with millions and millions of dollars, you only need one guy with a couple hundred thousand to be one of your investors or whatever. Could be anybody. Anybody with an IRA could be a potential investor, correct?

On your level with apartments it might be a little different because you need a little more money, but anybody could be a private investor.

Chris   Yeah. We've raised that 18 million dollars with an average investment of anywhere between 60 and 100 thousand dollars. I only have two guys that have written a check for a million dollars out of that 18. We have over 200 active investors at any given point and over 300 investors that have invested with us in the last four years alone. That's why I say, marketing wise, you don't get 300 investors if you're not marketing constantly to attract those investors.

Chris's Productivity Tip:

It's a really simple one. You've probably heard it in every time management book that we've ever read or that we've listened to is time blocking and shut your email off when you're working on a project. Time blocking for me is the biggest thing. If I sit down and block out on my calendar two hours a day to tackle the most important project that we have going on, I get so much done in that two hours versus when I deviate from that plan and I try to just run all day long with my emails and phone calls and get a little bit done, a little bit done here and there. What I can do in two hours could take me a day to finish if I didn't block out those two hours with a time blocking.

For more information on Chris and his company visit:

www.eliteapartmentcoaching.com

Mike Wolf

Mike has almost a quarter century of real estate investing experience and he and his team have been responsible for thousands of real estate transactions across the U.S. and Canada. Mike has been featured on NBC, ABC, CBS, Yahoo Finance, he's an international speaker, mentor, and leading authority on tax liens and deed investing and we are happy to have him with us here today.

Mike's Answer:

Well, that's a great question and I wish I knew 24 years ago what I know today because a lot of what I did was very much trial and error. I tried a whole bunch of things and luckily I had more good than bad and so I'm still luckily in the industry at this point. I'll give you a few pointers. One, I would've got a mentor much earlier on than I did. When I first started I actually got really lucky. My first deal was actually a very successful one where I actually made 6 figures. It took about 2 1/2 years to do it, but I made 6 figures on it. After I'd done that deal, I thought, "Man, this is easy." I started to get pretty cocky and confident in myself and the second deal I actually did went quite well, too. Not quite as good as that. I didn't have that kind of profit on the second deal, but I still did okay. By the third deal I thought I knew it all, I didn't need any help from anybody. I had it all dialed in and I took a significant loss on the third one.

One of the things I would recommend first of all is always have a mentor because when you become a know-it-all, that's when you're going to be handed a lesson and real estate lessons are very expensive. That's one of my first pointers for everybody is have somebody who's already paved the path before you, they've got the GPS and the road map and they can help you avoid those costly mistakes. Don't be a know-it-all, be a learn-it-all, and as you know, we always lead at a lot of different events where I'm still learning. After all these years I'm still learning how to do things better, whether it be my marketing, whether it be branding. Whatever it is, you got to keep learning. That's a little pointer. In terms of actual strategy, if I knew 24 years ago about tax deeds, that's what I would be doing and specifically in Texas.

I'll talk a little bit about that. For people who don't know what a tax deed is, when somebody hasn't paid their property taxes for 3 or 4 years, eventually the county has to put that home up for auction. Especially these days all across the U.S. there's cities going back bankrupt. Detroit's going bankrupt, California's in trouble, all the states and cities a lot of them are struggling to make payroll. They can barely pay the wages of their police, their fire, and all the government employees. They need these property tax dollars in order to keep current and keep with payroll. Eventually they put these homes up for auction and they put them up for auction for the amount typically owing on the back taxes. In Houston, Texas, which is my favorite place to use this strategy, we see single family homes going for $10,000 that are worth 6, 7, 8 times that. We see condos going for 3 and $4000 and we see vacant pieces of land, some lots, going for probably less than I spent on breakfast this morning. There's a lot of margin on these properties.

Now having said that, you do have to get educated on how to do the strategy properly because there are a lot of pitfalls. What will happen is I see a lot of people go in there, they don't really know what they're doing they just have dollar signs in their eyes, and they go there and they get properties and they don't know about all these things that can go wrong. It's very important to learn how to do the strategy properly but once you do that, it's a great way and you were mentioning if you had little or no money to start. If somebody's listening in on this and they've got millions of dollars to start, they can do this strategy, too, but you're going to have to do a lot more advancing.

If you're just starting out, one of the keys is you're going to have to raise capital somehow and the beauty of this strategy is one, as I mentioned, you don't need a lot of money, very very small amounts of money. But number two, when you become an expert at something that most other people don't know how to do well, it gives you a lot of leverage and ability to find other investors to finance your deals for you. What I mean by that, think of a doctor. A specialist will always make more money than a generalist. If you're a doctor, if you're a general practitioner, you're going to make certain amounts of money. If you're a plastic surgeon or an anesthesiologist, you make a whole lot more money. It's the same thing in real estate. When you know how to do something very specialized, your value goes up immensely very quickly.

I'll give you an example. I had a client of mine who, she called me up and she said, "Mike, I want to come on your," I do a tour, by the way, I do a 4-day mentorship in Houston, Texas. She said, "I want to come on your tour, but I have very little money. Does it make sense for me to come on your tour and learn the strategy?" I asked her what she did for a living and she goes, "dental hygienist." I said, "Well, let me ask you this. The dentist that you work for, do you think he would shut down his office, travel to Texas, spend several days driving around looking at properties, sit on the auction steps and first of all he'd have to learn how to do the strategy in the first place. Do you think he would ever do that?" She goes, "No, that wouldn't be a good use of his time."

I go, "Exactly, so what if you were to learn the strategy, go approach him and say, hey I'm not looking for large amounts of money. If you're able to invest 10 or 15,000 we can get started and I'll do all the work and we'll split the profits." That's exactly what she did. Of course she made him money, didn't take up any of his time. Time is very valuable to you if you're a dentist, a doctor, a lawyer, if you're anybody who's got some kind of really crazy busy career. The one thing they lack the most isn't usually the money, it's the time. She basically has the education, she has the time and the other thing I do is I give my clients a team. I have a team on the ground in Houston so that you don't actually have to fly to Texas ever again if you don't want to. I've got people that will go and view the properties for you, they'll check title, they'll actually go bid on your behalf at the auction and so her job really became not to learn the strategy and go do the work herself. Her job became to go raise money and call the team. Raise more money, call the team.

What ended up happening was she made this dentist some money. Of course he then wanted to invest much larger amounts, so it started off as a very small amount, then he wanted to invest much larger amounts. Not only that, what happens is, who do dentists go golfing with? They go golfing with other dentists. Now she's got other dentists phoning her up, saying, "Hey, I've got X amount of dollars, can you help me the way you helped Dr. So-and-so." Really the key is one, to summarize, is to have a good mentor who can teach you how to do things properly. Number two is learn a strategy. It doesn't have to be this one but make sure you know the strategy inside-out. One of the biggest mistakes I see investors making, and I did this too, is they want to try everything. They want to learn how to do 10 different things at once and they try to be a jack of all trades and what ends up happening is you do a whole bunch of things very mediocre and that doesn't really add any value.

Imagine you went to an investing meet-up, a real estate investor meet-up. You went in there and said, "My name is Mike and I'm a real estate investor and I'm going to be looking for properties on the MLS, will you fund my deals?" Everybody's going to say, "Well we have access to the MLS. You're not really providing any value." That's the key is to provide value. On the other hand, you go to that meeting, you say, "Hey, I'm Mike Wolf, I specialize in Texas tax deeds. I've got a team on the ground. Here's our track record of deals that we've done." I encourage my students all the time to say this is what the team has done. You never want to lie and say you've done a deal you didn't do, but the same team that's helped all my other students get these deals with great results is the same team you're going to be using. You can say, "Hey these are some of the deals that the team has done."

Now, one you're satisfying their biggest fear is am I going to get my money back? They're not worried about the returns; they're worried am I going to get my money back at all? That satisfies that. Secondly you're showing them; hey it's not going to take up your time. You don't need to be an expert at this. You don't need to do anything. All you have to do is cut a check and the rest of it's going to fall into place. For somebody who's starting off with very little money, I would recommend doing a couple of flips in that market to have some more capital and then you can continue to use other people's money but you'll also have some of your money that you can do not only this strategy but you can start to do deals as you get more and more money the options open up to you. The world opens up to you and you'll have a lot more possibilities at that point.

That's exactly what I would do if I was starting fresh today. I wish I had known about it because the strategy actually has been around for over 200 years. As long as there's been property taxes, the government's always had a way to collect delinquent taxes. 24 years ago when I started it was available, but I had no clue. It wasn't on my radar, wouldn't have a clue how to do it. But that would be my advice for anybody starting fresh is to find a strategy that's one, lucrative, two, adds value to somebody else. It's a lot easier to find somebody who's got money sitting in their bank than to try and save up money to do it yourself. Get used to using other people's money as early as possible.

That's another big lesson. It took a long time before I had the confidence to ever ask anybody if they wanted to fund my deals for me. If I could go back in time that's one of the things I would've done much earlier because I would have had a much quicker start. Not that I'm complaining. Everything worked out pretty good, but I could've had a quicker start, had a little bit more velocity, and eventually if you want to keep doing bigger and bigger deals, you are going to have to use other people's money no matter what. The sooner you start doing it, the better off you're going to be and always remember that when you're doing this you're not asking to borrow money. What you're doing is creating an opportunity for somebody, adding value to them, and taking a lose-lose, like in the case of the dentist.

His money was sitting in his bank doing nothing and he didn't have time to learn how to invest it wisely. He didn't have a clue how to get started with it and so she took what she knew and she didn't have any money. She took a loss for her, she had a strategy but no money, she couldn't do a deal. He had money and he also couldn't do a deal, and together they created a win-win. That's really the key. Create win-wins wherever you go and the rest of it will fall into place and you'll have a great real estate career as long as you keep that on your mind at all times. Everything you do has to be a win-win and you've got to add value to whoever you're working with.

Jim: That's great. Just to recap a bit, obviously get a mentor early on which is key. I'm sure you still have them. I still have them in my life. I've been doing this only 7 years, I don't have 24 years under my belt, but I always have mentors, I always will and I always just like you said, you continue learning always. I spend money on education up to $20,000 a year, masterminds and traveling to seminars to learn more and do stuff and I'm sure you still do the same thing. I see you at them so I know you do.

Mike: Yeah, absolutely. It's huge.

Jim: A really great tip that you gave here is like you said tax deeds are a great opportunity, specifically Texas, but not even if tax deeds aren't for you in Texas because that's something you just think that's not for me, but to specialize on one specific thing. Pick something and learn it really, really well. Don't be as the saying goes, a jack of all trades but master of nothing where you know a little bit about everything but in this business, real estate investing, you can get burned. You can lose money here. If you really get a specialized, if you learn something very well and you can add value to lots of people with it, that's very powerful stuff.

The thing about the dentist with that particular story, it's a take away for everybody listening is you never know who a private lender could be. Don't overthink private lenders. All a private lender is somebody you know that has money in the bank. It's not some big secret here. It could be your mom, your brother, your sister. It could be anybody that you know that has even an IRA that you can use as self-directed IRA or cash in the bank or if you have a dentist, doctor, whatever you have access to that has money sitting in the bank. Anybody could become a private lender.

Mike's Productivity Tip:

I think the biggest thing would be to block time. During that time focus on whatever it is you're doing and turn off the email, turn off the cellphone, turn off the text. Don't have any interruptions and give yourself a solid 2, 3 hours. Take little breaks in between but stay very focused because a lot of us real estate investors, we tend to have that entrepreneurial spirit and entrepreneurs are very guilty, including myself, of having Shiny Object Syndrome. We lose our focus and we have too many things distracting us.

If you just have time at one point in the day, whatever time works for you where you just are strictly focused on what you do and don't let anybody interrupt that time, everything else will fall into place a lot better because if you divide it up where you're doing 15 minutes here and then you get caught up in your emails, then you do 15 minutes there and you start texting somebody, 15 minutes there. I like having a straight solid work time. This works a lot better, you're going to get a lot better results. You're going to have a lot more clarity and you're going to get your results a lot quicker because your attention doesn't get diffused.

For more information on Mike and get some of his free training videos visit: www.MikeWolfMastery.com

Tucker Merrihew

Tucker Merrihew. Tucker started off in the real estate business as a loan officer back in 2002. Then in 2005, this guy opened his own mortgage company. He had done a decent amount of real estate investing during that time as a loan officer, then a mortgage broker, but in 2008, after we had the real estate crash, he transitioned his focus onto building his development company, which is TTM Development Company. They started out doing wholesaling and rehabbing in pretty large numbers. Their primary source for deals was auctions and bank foreclosures. They were doing REOs, short sales, and auction stuff. Then in 2010, Tucker began mastering the art of finding more deeply discounted deals through direct marketing to private sellers to buy their properties directly from them.

Today, Tucker runs one of the biggest real estate investment companies in the Portland, Oregon, area and he's host of an extremely popular podcast called The Real Dealz Podcast. It can be found on iTunes or at www.The Real Dealz Podcast.com. That's Dealz with a Z.

Tucker's Answer:

I tell you what, it would be … I'd try and make it as simple as possible. I think a lot of times people try to overcomplicate this business, and it's really a very simple business, at least from the outside. That is, you need to find properties that should be bought at a discount or should at some point sell to an investor. The best way that I feel to do that and the most cost efficient way to do that is to utilize what I call driving for dollars. Essentially, what that means is you identify certain neighborhoods or areas that you want to have as your farm area or areas that you're going to continue to market to on an ongoing basis, and you either drive those areas and write down the addresses of homes that appear to need a lot of work, or if you're a cheapskate and you don't want to pay for gas, you can actually walk around those areas as well.

There are actually a couple of different neighborhoods that we invest in pretty heavily in my market of Portland, Oregon. I've walked every street in those neighborhoods for … I've got two big English mastiff dogs and they need to be walked every now and again, so I'd actually drive the neighborhood and then walk the dogs up and down the streets and I'd write down all the addresses for homes that appear to either need some major renovation or updating, repair. You generally want to target homes that are run down with bad roofs, rotted siding, overgrown landscaping, roller ramps up to the front door, trash in the yard, blue tarps on the roof or on all kinds of things on the home. They usually stand out like a sore thumb. We'd drive, walk around, bike around, whatever you want to do around these neighborhoods that you identify and get those addresses written down, try and start to build a list.

Then another niche that we also focus on is in the mid-range to upper price point neighborhoods. It's that same strategy, but we'll also include smaller homes, like two-bedroom, one-bath types of homes in the higher end areas because those homes are good candidates for either the knock-down, new-build strategy where somebody can knock them down and then build a nicer, newer, bigger house in that area or they can add on to the existing house by adding a little more square footage and ultimately being able to sell the house for a lot more money that way.

Those are the different types of houses that we look for, but, of course, in order to get the marketing campaigns going for that, you need to write down the addresses and then you need to go through the process of locating, okay, where does the owner live, what's their name, do they live at that property, do they live somewhere else. Create that list and then that there is basically real estate gold because it's a list that not every investor will do. Most people want to hit the easy button, buy a list, go to Click2Mail, send out postcards, and hope that somebody calls and then make a million dollars flipping a house.

There's a little more work involved in this strategy, but by doing so, you're getting a highly, highly targeted potential lead, probably the highest, the most highly targeted lead that you can get because you've actually looked at the house and it passes the sniff test of, okay, this house is going to need to sell to an investor at some point. It's not a house that's best suited for the retail market, or it's a house where the land is actually worth more than the house that's on it currently. That would make for a good candidate for a knock-down, new-build type strategy.

Once you're able to locate who owns the house and where they live, then you want to design a marketing campaign to try and get those people to reach out to you and contact you. You haven't spent much money in creating this list if you're walking around, driving around, writing down these addresses and then looking up who owns them and where they live. It's pretty minimal. You can continue that theme of having a minimal expense by then creating a handwritten marketing campaign to these addresses that you've written down and sending them to the owners of each property.

One thing I would suggest is doing a handwritten note of some sort. Then what we will do and what I would suggest anybody else does in order to try and spur a response from these people is to send them two or three handwritten notes over the course of a six- to eight-week period of time. That way, you're getting in front of them enough that it gives you the highest likelihood that they're going to pick up the phone and give you a call.

Obviously, timing is kind of the most important key to this. People have to be at least thinking about the idea of selling their home at the same time that they receive one of your marketing pieces, so you may not get a call right off from people, but that doesn't mean that they won't call you eventually. At the same time, if you do enough of these, you'll get people that are thinking about selling and they'll call you right off, so you can start to fill out your pipeline of deals. You've got your more immediate deals and then as you continue to market and you continue to be in the business, those people that maybe timing wasn't right at that point in time, they may call you in the future, and then, boom, you've got a potential deal there as well.

At the same time that you're kind of building out your list that you're marketing to, you also want to figure out, okay, what your exit strategy is going to be. If you're new in the business and you don't have a whole lot of money and a whole lot of experience, chances are you're probably going to be looking to wholesale these properties as opposed to renovating them or building a new home yourself. That's fine; that's a good place to start.

At the same time that you're marketing this list, you also want to pay close attention to that same area and look and see what you can find as far as sales over the course of the past year and any current construction projects that are also going on in that neighborhood. By doing that, you're essentially trying to find the real players in your market, the guys that are really buying, really doing deals, really doing the construction whether it be just renovations, add-on renovations, or knock-down, new-build type strategies.

One thing that a lot of investors do that they get stuck on is they'll go to the extent of finding out who these people are, and then they'll send them a letter. They don't get any response, so they think, well, they're not interested in buying anything from me. That's not the case at all. Generally, these people are extremely busy and they just have a hard time finding the time to pick up the phone to talk to you about a potential deal. On top of that, they probably get a fair bit of newbie-type investors that send them letters saying that they have inventory in the neighborhood that they're working in and they'd love to talk to them about selling it to them. People have seen that so much now that they don't put a whole lot of stock in it being valid.

What I would suggest doing is figure out who these real players are, these real buyers are. Find out what their phone number is, what their company name is. Give them a call, talk to them, meet with them, figure out what it is that they're looking to buy, what's their sweet spot, what's their wheelhouse, how much they're paying for lots, how much they're paying for add-on rehab projects, how much they're paying for surface rehab projects in any given area. Then you've got an order to fill. All you do at that point is then continue your marketing campaign towards these potential properties that could be a deal, and then you're just filling orders for those real players that you've built relationships with. That would be-

Jim: Just to carry on about what you said. I want the people listening to ... about reaching out to the cash buyers in your markets. Because a lot of people will be beginning. They're listening to this or reading this. For me in my market, I have guys that reach out to me. I'm a rehabber in Chicago, so I have guys that reach out to me on a weekly basis, just like I'm sure you do, Tucker. I don't call them back because there are so many new ones. I do my marketing in my area, and I'm pretty well-known in my markets. It's not hard to find who the players are. Once you're one of those, you're going to get contacted. I don't even call them back until the third time

	they've called me. If they only call me once, they're not getting a call back from me. I'm not being rude there. I'm weeding out weak ones.
Tucker:	You're absolutely right. There's a lot of noise out there, especially when you're in a position like me, a position like you, where you're pretty well-known and you're pretty easy to find in your market as somebody who's doing a lot of whether it be renovation, new construction, add-on renovation projects, so there's a lot of people that will try and contact you. Usually, they do that through sending letters. Some will get a little bolder and maybe they call you every once in awhile. You have to be that guy that basically is not going to not connect with them. You're going to be that guy that says, look, I need to get coffee, a meeting, come to their office, and talk to them. Figure out that you've got matching personalities, you guys can do business. Then on top of that, also figure out what it is exactly that they're looking to buy so that you can fill that order.
Jim:	Yeah, for sure. The reason I don't call back or if I get one letter ... Again, I'm not being rude;

it's to weed out the weak. I want the guy who's going to call me three times, like hey, I need to come in your office. I need to meet with you, the aggressive one. Because it's a hard enough business to make it in. The average sale, they say, of anything is made between the fifth and twelfth contact. If you're only reaching out four times, you haven't even made it to when the average sale is made for whatever you're trying to accomplish. Right?

Tucker: That's right. You're also able to tell then, okay, on your side of the coin, who is it that really has the stick-to-itiveness and the drive to actually make me have a conversation with them. Because those are the same people that will actually end up also following up with sellers enough in order to put a deal together for me to buy. You're weeding them out at the same time because you don't want to waste your time or theirs, and if it's just going to be a hobby for somebody for the next few weeks, you don't need to meet with them, have coffee with them, talk to them, and waste your time.

Jim: Which is the majority that call you, quite frankly, because most never do a deal.

Tucker: You're right. Absolutely. I've talked to more bird dogs, let's say, than I can count over the years, and I think one of the hundreds that we talk to … Usually, we get a big influx any time a big seminar comes into town over the course of the next couple of weeks after that. We've had one bird dog ever that's actually delivered a viable deal. That just kind of shows that there's not as much stick-to-itiveness as there should be in this business. If you can commit yourself to treat this like a business and stick to it, it will work. It's just you have to have faith in the process and you have to have faith in the business. A lot of people lose that along the way or they lose their motivation for whatever reason.

Now the strategy that I just mentioned there's a large human element to that strategy, whether it be sourcing the deals or whether it be selling the deals to whoever the rehabber or the builder is going to be. The human element is something that trips a lot of people up. A lot of people just want to sit by on a computer screen, make offers on HUD homes, make offers on REOs, having agents do work for them, or going to the auction and bidding on a property or having a bidding service bid on it for you. There's no human element there. They're able to sit in their comfort zone and not have to master the art of engaging in that human element. That kind of separates the men from the boys a little bit and the people that really want to commit themselves to be a good sales person, be a good people person, and put themselves out there and put in the work.

But at the same time, if you're able to do that and you do commit yourself to that and you're able to kind of embrace the human element side of the business, ultimately you can write your own paycheck and you can experience the freedom and the financial upside that this business can present to everybody.

Jim: Let me take you back here. The handwritten note that you send, is that literally a handwritten note or is it a handwritten print? Are you guys literally doing a handwritten note?

Tucker: No. I'm a big advocate of not doing the printed handwritten fonts. It's pretty minimal cost, and especially if you're doing a driving-for-dollars campaign, usually those lists are fairly small. It's a very targeted list. Each property is one that actually should be bought by an investor at some point or a builder. I feel like you should really put a little more time, effort, and money into your mailers that you're sending to that list and that would include actually sending them a handwritten note as opposed to some sort of printed version. There's some out there that are pretty decent, but as soon as somebody kind of starts to question whether it's real or whether it's printed, they may not have the confidence in you that they would otherwise to give you a call and that skepticism meter starts to kick in. You want to keep that skepticism meter at bay as much as you can.

Jim: Yeah. I couldn't agree more. I just was curious, because depending on how many you're doing. Yeah, I've had a lot of success with handwritten notes. I had my assistant doing it for years, and she hated that. Still, it was very effective. You can tell. If it's a printed one, exactly what you said, they're skeptical. Is this just a big bulk campaign? Who am I even going to get on the phone? When they can tell it's handwritten, they can tell the difference, they realize they're going to get somebody on the phone who is the real investor who is going to buy it. That's more fear and-

Tucker: Yeah. We actually bought a number of homes over the years where I've looked at the other marketing pieces that people have received and there have occasionally been ones where people actually printed handwritten font and the sellers have told me that they called me over them because they thought it was some sort of a scammer. They were very skeptical of it because they could tell that it was likely printed and not handwritten. One of the things that we do, obviously, we like to write a ton of handwritten notes. It's a real pain in the you-know-what, so we actually hire letter-writers in our office. Our letter-writers actually do all of that writing for us, and that's their job every day is to just crank those out.

Tucker's Productivity Tip:

I would say this is actually a tool that we've been building ourselves for my own business over the course of the last year, year and a half. We will be completed with it and it will be available for everybody in the real estate investment world as of February of 2015. What that is, it's a driving-for-dollars app that actually can be installed on your iPhone or your Android phone. Basically, what it does for you is all of the heavy lifting and research that goes into creating these custom lists. All that heavy lifting, research time, those are barriers of entry for a lot of solopreneur investors that maybe just are having a hard time finding the time or the energy in order to build those lists. Because it does take time, it does take effort. It's something that a lot of people say, ah, you know what, I'll just buy this list instead because I don't have to go put in the work.

This app, it's called the driving-for-dollars app, and it can be found on Driving for Dollars App.com. We'll also be talking about it a lot on The Real Dealz Podcast coming up over the course of the next month or so. Basically, what it does for you is you go through a neighborhood, you identify any given house, and it will store the picture, it will store the address, it will pull the owner's information, the address of where they live, will compile the list in a format that you can then export, mail merge, put your mailers together, mailing campaign, whatever. It does virtually everything for you that's kind of the pain-in-the-butt part of building a list like that.

Jim: Wow. That's awesome. I've never heard of anything like that. I've driven for dollars. Every neighborhood I'm in, still today, I'm always looking, writing down addresses, sending them letters. That would make it a whole lot easier. I'm looking forward to when ... You said it will be done in February?

Tucker: It will be done in February. Again, it was something that we started building for my own business because if you have a larger business like myself or you, you've got labor costs, time costs of not only building a list but then researching and getting all the data that you need to mail the list. Then if you're a solopreneur, it's just hard to find the time. This kind of removes those barriers of entry and those costs, those labor costs that are associated with creating custom marketing lists.

For more information on Tucker and his company visit:

www.TTMDevelopmentCompany.com

Or on The Real Dealz Podcast

ERIK STARK

Erik is just thirty one years old and he has already bought, flipped, sold over 400 properties in The last seven years.

Now in addition to that he holds a very nice portfolio of single family, multifamily and commercial rental properties.

Now the interesting thing about Erik is about a year ago, he and his wife of twelve years decided to up and move his family down to warmer climates from the Detroit market he was in, or just North of Detroit, to an oceanside community in South Florida.

He had a lot of success up there in Detroit, decided to move down to Florida into paradise and Build another business down there. This is a perfect roll into the question for today especially since you just did that in Florida can you let us know what you did when you moved there?

Erik: Absolutely, that's exactly what we did ironically enough is we picked up, moved down here and just duplicated what we did in Michigan and essentially just shaved off the excess fluff that wasn't really contributing to our goal.

So as soon as we got down here, the first thing we did was **gauge the market**. Find out where all the **major** activity is, we knew where we wanted to spend the time at and that was focusing on **quality versus quantity.** We no longer wanted to be the guys that were doing fifty, sixty, seventy, a hundred deals a year ... we want to get down to doing twenty-five or less.

So we focused on where the activity was, pulled up the heat maps, found out where all the cash sales were going on, a lot of the new construction ... **where the big opportunities were** at is **where the majority of people weren't**. I think this goes with any market, is that when you just play in that low end, easily obtainable, saturated market which is usually the landlord areas, mid-market flips or cheap wholesale deals, that's where you're finding the majority of people are spending their time, making it the most competitive market in any city.

We chose to do the direct opposite and go after that higher end market where it's a little bit more risky, much less competitive but the returns are a lot greater.

We had to gauge the market for hot activity and get in front of the market. Ever since we moved to Florida we put the philosophy together, since we spend a lot of time fishing here so whenever you go out on a fishing boat the captain's asking, "what do want to do? You want to catch fish or are you out here to relax?"

If you're here to relax, grab a cold one, drop a line in the water and just enjoy your day. If you're here to catch fish, get six lines running bait them and let's go get in front of the reefs, drop our lines and just start scooping people up. The same philosophy applies to real estate. Go where the activity is and drop as many lines as you can.

Jim: When you went to Florida, what did you focus on or how did you start? Where did you start? I know you said the heat maps and so you focused where people actually weren't going.

So how did you decide to do that and what's the angle there?

Erik: It's not that we went where people weren't going. We went where the majority weren't going. This was a quality over quantity decision so I guess what I mean by that is it's very hard to do without being in the streets. The MLS, mailing, online leads, they are all worked by the majority and very few people actually play in the streets where the immediate activity is. That's where we like to play and that is where we REALLY learn what is going on in the market. Just like numbers don't lie, the streets don't lie.

Zillow, Trulia, the MLS and Realtors can only tell me so much because when I get out into the streets, which I typically do every single day, I'm

> out verifying what is going on, talking to ACTIVE buyers, sellers, and lenders of real estate.

Every day.

That's what makes up our market activity is to be out there talking with people that are actually doing the activity, not the ones that are usually sitting behind a computer screen talking about that activity.

So we just started driving around with a yellow pad of paper.

Stopping at every construction site, stopping at every dilapidated property and just kind of kept going the direction that a lot of people weren't.

When I came down here, we went to all the networking events, all the REIA's, talked with as many people as we could and we found that everybody's playing in that lower end wholesale markets feeding these hedge funds these properties. But their margins are so thin because there's so many people attacking them all at the same time, we went to where there's activity but on a much less competitive level.

The only way that we were able to do that is once you have your general idea and the overview of where the market is at, activity wise, you get out in the streets and you verify and you say yes, this is where I want to start spending my time.

When we did come down here, we focused on Pareto's law, the 80/20 rule. Look at where the activity's coming from, shave off what we don't need and let's go hard after what's making a difference in our lives.

Quick Example: We could chase $5000 wholesale deals with ease and set up an operation in 60 days. We will be fighting over $5k paydays with the rest of the market and use a TON of energy and resources to do so. Or, we can focus on BIG oppty, like the building market. We find a builder looking for a 8000 sq. ft. lot for $750,000 and begin working backwards to find him a lot. So we have a built in buyer, are learning the builders marketplace and essentially, anything we get it for under $750,000 per 8000 sq. ft. is our fee. Less competition, bigger margins, less risk and it's in an area of such great demand; it's truly prestigious just to be able to play oceanside. As where wholesaling is typically done in low end, war zone areas.

We still do a lot of direct mail. Absentees are obviously the most flooded marketing you could ever do. But we certainly don't ignore it. We just don't bank on absentees. You still pull good leads off of absentees and the secret with that is consistency.

So when we got down here, we immediately set up what worked for us well in Michigan and that was direct mail.

1. We pulled our HIGHLY FILTERED and DOUBLE CLEANED absentees

2. We built a list of over 1000 driving for dollars and distressed looking, ugly properties, especially in the higher end neighborhoods

3. We got our probates set up

4. We met with all the city field inspectors letting them know we want to help clean up the neighborhoods (something

that magically happens when you drive the streets all day. Try cold calling these guys and see how far you get.

Then we started to spend a lot of time at networking events letting people know exactly what we're looking to purchase. Attorneys, city meetings, Realtors. People who are just outside of our industry but indirectly involved.

So from having three-five different sources of marketing going on, getting out in the networking to three events every week and then spending every single day in the field looking at properties and writing offers, those few things done consistently, build a great pipeline relatively quickly.

Jim: So you go to three REIA type events a week? Is that what I'm gathering?

Erik: We don't go to a lot of REIA events; we go to events that are just on the outskirts of real estate. Maybe a marketing or entrepreneurial or a raising capital kind of event. We attend city hall meetings, men's groups and those still in our industry but indirectly related.

The last thing we want to do is be saturated repeatedly in the same kind of room where other people are trying to accomplish the same thing. If you notice the main pattern of ours, it's to be silently capitalizing on the markets biggest opportunities, without being directly involved with the masses and without make a large ripple that will attract attention in our direction.

In this new economy we are in, marketing just needs to be a given, it needs to be there, it needs to be operating but you MUST be out prospecting for more business every day because you're not just dropping a marketing campaign and getting a flood of leads, we're still getting great responses but a lot of sellers they pin us against each other.

I truly do not tell ANYONE this but this was one of the major breakthroughs for us in Michigan so we immediately put it into action down here.

Here in Florida, I've been fortunate enough to meet a mentor who hands me over every single marketing piece he receives, and so far, there's sixty four other people marketing to absentee owners.

I cannot emphasize how critical this was to our success but think about it. When you can arm yourself with the knowledge of what your competition is doing, you see what they're mailing, how frequently, what kind of message, what style medium are they using … is it a postcard, is it a letter, is it a flyer … when you're able to gauge that level of activity, it really puts you one step ahead because you're able to be more consistent, you're able to make a mailer that's totally different than what the rest of everybody else is doing and you're kind of able to step up to the plate because you're armed with the knowledge of what your competitors are doing.

As marketers we know, the money is in the data. That data is crucial to us and that has been a monumental business breakthrough for us.

Erik's Productivity Tip:

That's a great question Jim.

There is a lot that goes into building a productive life and essentially, I strongly feel, if you are not connected to YOUR WHY (the reason you do this) it's hard to be hyper focused and productive in all you're doing so here is some things that contribute to our productivity.

- **Wake Up Early** (like 4am early and focus on YOU during that time)

- Know WHY you do this and guard it like IT MATTERS more than anything, because it does.

- Have weekly **What Matters** list that the family knows about–I sit with my wife and son every Sunday and ask what matters to them this week. That way I know that I am meeting my wife for lunch Tuesday, playing basketball with my son these two nights and can flow through life and not miss (or be late) for what matters MOST.

- **Non Negotiable Actions**-In this business, we get sideswiped with tasks all day long. When I week-Takeknow that my main to do list is Add More Buyers, Sellers and Lenders to my appointments this week. This builds a default around my most demanding actions and if they don't meet up to this level of activity, I don't deal with it.

- **Brain Dump** once per week–Take 5 minutes and write down EVERYTHING that comes to mind during that time. Cross off that which you cannot do anything about and handle that which you can. This clears your mental desk to be more productive. Finish your undone tasks so you are not operating at half efficiency.

- **Practice the 80/20 rule** ridiculously. My wife hates this part about me at times but if I have ANYTHING in life that takes away from my 20% more than once, it gets brain dumped and usually outsourced or left undone. I just have built a sick level of intolerance for mundane activity in my life.

- **Celebrate Life.** One thing I have done a lot more of down here is to celebrate life. Biking and working out are no longer dreaded activities of mine. It's a form of celebrating this great life I live and recognizing it as a blessing not a curse. This ties into my BIG WHY and brings it full circle but dammit, since we work hard, we play hard too.

FOCUS ON WHAT MATTERS. To me, my family matters.

I don't know if that's a productivity tool but I know me mentally, when I know that I'm waking up… and even if I give four hours of my absolute best versus the guy that gives ten hours of average mediocrity, I think your average still winds up better when you're focusing on the quality of life, quality of business, quality of activity versus the guy that just says I'm out here just trying to get as many things on the wall as I can and let's just see what sticks.

For more information on Erik you can find him on Facebook:

therealerikstark@facebook.com

Ian Flannigan

Ian is the founder of Freedom Investing Academy and co-founder of Golden Falls Properties. Now these guys are doing about 10 to 15 transactions a month, leveraging debt without using any of their own money and they're teaching their students how to do it and that's what they did it, Freedom Investing Academy. Now they're out of Dallas, Texas market. They've been doing this stuff for about 9 years and we're very happy to have him on the call with us.

Ian's Answer:

Well, that's actually a great question. I'm glad you asked it. There are so many things that can consume your time when you're first starting out and trying to get a business off the ground. The very first thing that I would do is I would focus on building cash flow just so I wasn't chasing all these transactional deals because the great thing about putting cash flow deals together is you do the deal one time and you keep getting paid over and over and over each and every month. With that said, the marketing strategy that I would focus on would be I would market for tenant buyers.

People that are looking to buy property either on a lease option or some type of seller financing agreement where they could make a large down payment or a significant down payment upfront and then balance them out with monthly payments. Putting together those types of cash flow deals where you can control real estate through a lease option or a subject to or something like that and then turning around and sandwiching yourself in between the spread and bringing in that buyer. Focusing on building a buyers list first because if you don't have inventory, you can go directly to other investors in your market once you have a buyers list and you can really tap into it that way.

Jim: What you say to find tenant buyers or build a buyers list. If you don't have a lot of cash in the beginning and you're starting out to become an investor, what's a good way to build that buyers list without having much money? What would you do?

Ian: Well, the greatest invention in the world is the Internet. That the first place that I would go. Craig's List is a great resource for investors. We call them ghost ads. Opening up several e-mail accounts so ... You can only post one ad through one e-mail account so opening up 7 different e-mail accounts and every 2 to 3 hours, going on and putting a ghost ad on Craig's List saying that you have a property for sale with owner financing or lease option, whatever your message is.

Start building a database of those buyers that are looking to buy properties that have cash. They may have some beat up credit but that's okay. We can work with that. Start building a list of buyers that are looking to buy with a down payment and balance [them 03:05] monthly. That would be the first thing that I would do is jump on Craig's List and also you have the other social media platforms. You can do marketing through Facebook and other channels as well. Being able to put the marketing out there for free on the Internet is the first thing that I would do starting over.

Yes absolutely we find buyers and sellers on Craigslist. If you look in the major metropolitan markets, you'll see a ton of ads that investors are actually putting up there that they have property for sale with owner financing. If you can contact an investor when you know you have a buyers list and just simply say to him, "Hey, would you joint venture with me if I can bring buyers to you? Would you consider splitting the down payments if they close on the properties?" Anytime someone can bring me a buyer and I can close a property very fast, I don't have any problems paying them a fee or splitting a down payment with that other party to get the deal done so I can go on and do another one.

Jim: On these lease options subject to ... What you're saying you're talking about splitting this down payment. That's like what you'd call a non-refundable option money. Is that how you're getting paid on these deals just so the people that are listening understand.

Ian: Yeah, absolutely. For example, let's say an investor has a property for sale for $200,000. He's selling it with a lease option. You've been doing some marketing. You have some ghost ads. You have a buyers list of folks that have cash. Let's say they have $20,000. Now, you can call that investor up that has that property and say, "Look, I have a buyer that has $20,000 cash. If my buyer wants your property, what can we negotiate on a fee to pay me for bringing the buyer?" You don't want to be too greedy upfront. Fifty-fifty would be a lot considering the investor is looking to maximize as much as he can out of the down payment, but if I can bring him a buyer that can pay him $15,000 and pay me 5 then I think that would be a win-win for all parties involved.

Absolutely. Yeah. That's inventory that's already on the market. Most people don't really take that approach.

Jim: For a new investor that would probably be a great place to start too. Go to find the guys that already have the deals and just market their deals for them. I mean you probably have to call them and make sure that's okay.

Ian: Yes, you absolutely would, but like I was saying if you start by building the database of buyers, it makes it a lot easier to have that conversation with an investor that has a property for sale.

Ian's Productivity Tip:

Communication. The networking and communication with other professionals. I think a lot of people in the beginning they're a little gun shy. You're scared to talk to people just because they don't have the knowledge or the language to speak real estate so it's very critical to start building those relationships. I like to tell people this, even my clients. This entire business is all about communication and paperwork. That's how the business of real estate is done.

Even if you're borrowing money from private lenders or you're getting sellers to accept your offer or you're selling properties to buyers, there's always a bit of communication there. If you're not speaking to people on a weekly basis, making those outbound phone calls, going to those real estate networking events, you're never going to get the business off the ground. That was what really turned the corner for me years ago was starting to build relationships with other professionals.

I leveraged their credibility as long as I could to help get me to where I wanted to go. The one habit that I would say is communication with other professionals through outbound phone calls, calling people, just calling other investors that have properties for sale and just having a conversation with them. Ask them what they're looking for. The next time you see something come across your desk or e-mail, you know you have a couple guys or a handful of guys that are looking for specific properties. Just simply making those phone calls and just talking to other professionals. Building the relationships with other guys and women in the business is very very critical.

Jim: You can look at that as networking for deals. Right? I mean it doesn't get much more inexpensive than that to potentially put deals together if it's just talking. Right?

Ian: Absolutely. Yeah. It's just building that relationship. All the investors are looking for deals. They all have their little niche here and there. I can't say that enough. Is building relationships with other professionals and just that communication whether it be just sitting from your house, your home, your work, in between work. I used to make phone calls on my lunch breaks in the morning. Just making those phone calls and then going to those meetings. Just opening that dialogue with other professionals and really start building a database of other professionals that you can turn to put deals together.

Ian has a free web class you can sign up for at:

www.freedominvestingacademy.com/gift

Joe McCall

Joe does wholesaling and he does wholesaling lease options. The coaching program where he teaches wholesalers how to … Wholesale lease options, he teaches them how to wholesale. You can find out more about this on his podcast at real estate investing mastery at his website which is realestateinvestingmastery.com. Now a quick story about Joe is this year, Joe wholesaled three … Six properties, I'm sorry, six properties from an RV while traveling the country with his family for two and a half months in three different markets.

This is the guy you want to hear what he has to say because obviously he's doing this while spending quality time with his family, which is something that's very important to all of us. Joe thank you for being here with us today.

Joe's Answer:

Well I'm going to bet you $100 I'm not the first one to tell you this. I would go after the buyers first. I would go find the buyers first and then find the deals for them. Without much money I would go into the MLS, I would probably scrape up as many pennies as I can find and go to a service like List Source or List Ability and I would do a search in my county for all of the cash buyers or the investors who purchased properties in the last six months. I would send them a letter, I'd send them a post card, I'd try to find their phone number, I'd knock on their door. I would see who were the players. See who are the ones who bought a lot of properties in the last six months, I'd get a hold of them, get them on the phone and I would just introduce myself to them. Start working on networking and building relationships with cash buyers.

Once you have the buyers, you know what they want, you know what kind of properties they're looking for, you know what the best zip codes are, you know what they'll pay for, and you'll know their minimum criteria. It just makes everything so much easier.

Jim: You're just reverse engineering the process, right? You're starting with the end goal of buyer and then find what they want and then you go get it for them and bring it back to them, right?

Joe: Exactly. It sounds so simple. It's almost easy. I've heard this many, many times as I was getting started in the business. At the time, I remember thinking, "Oh that just sounds too simple. Everybody's probably doing that." Or it didn't sound like ... I wanted something that sounded more complicated, for some reason, right?

Well, I don't know why I didn't really believe it when I first got started, so I did the traditional thing of find the sellers first and there's nothing wrong with that. I still do a ton of seller marketing. It was about a year and a half ago I was looking for a new acquisitions manager. I dusted off all of my wholesaling course because I wanted to train this guy. I didn't want to give him my stuff. I wanted to give him some other people's stuff. I found some stuff online about reverse wholesaling, about finding the buyers first. Then I started just sending postcards and letters for my acquisitions manager and I tasked him with finding these buyers. We didn't drive them to websites; we didn't try to get their email address. We just sent them a simple letter saying something along the lines of, "Hey, we're one of the premier wholesaling companies in the St. Louis area. We do a lot of deals. We have properties that give our investors 15 to 20% cash on cash returns. If you want more information, give us a call. We'd love to talk with you."

We sent that letter to all the recent buyers who bought properties in St. Louis. We also sent that letter to a lot of … There's probably … I mean, at the time there was about six or seven really hot markets where a lot of out of state investors were buying properties in these markets. Like Dallas, Atlanta, Memphis, Tennessee, Indianapolis, Cincinnati, Cleveland, Ohio. Markets like that. We found who were the most active investor buyers in those markets as well. Buying in those markets from out of state. We sent out about five hundred to a thousand letters, I don't remember. We got an okay response back. I was training my acquisitions manager to, "Look, when these guys call, drop everything you're doing, get on the phone, talk to them, and just build a relationship with them. Find out what they want. What are they looking for? What's their buying criteria? What do they want to avoid? What kind of properties are they looking for? Three bedrooms? Two bedrooms? Does it have to have a basement? Does it have to have a garage? What kind of rent do they want? What's the most they want to put into repairs?"

That's all this guy did for two months. We just marketed for buyers. We started building relationships with these guys. Really quickly we found about three or four really solid cash buyers and they had a ton of money and they're looking for more properties. We found out exactly what they're looking for. Then we started marketing. By that time too, we actually started calling all of the for rent properties that were in Zillow in our target areas. We let our buyers tell us where they wanted to buy, right? Then we looked up all of the properties that were listed for rent in Zillow and on Craigslist in those areas and we started calling the landlord, started calling the property managers and asking them if they had a property they wanted to sell. We told them, "Hey, we're in the market. We're looking to buy some more properties in this area. Would you client ... "If it's a property manager, we'd say, "Would your client have any interest in selling this property? Or do you have any other clients who'd be interested in selling their property?" We told that realtor or property manager, "Look, you can represent us; you can get both sides of the commission. We're looking for deals." We started spreading the word out. We started spreading the word that, "hey, we got two million dollars burning a hole in our pocket. We're looking for deals; we need deals in these markets."

As word started spreading around in St. Louis and pretty soon, we didn't have to do any seller marketing. We had about ten, twenty people every week were giving us leads, were giving us deals. We tied them up under contract; we double closed on them and sell them. We would sell them to our cash buyers. Anyways, make a short story long, we found that when you have the buyers first, it just makes everything so much easier because then you can start marketing for sellers with so much more confidence, knowing that you have the money to buy the property. Make sense Jim?

Jim: Yeah, absolutely. I mean, it's like anything ... With any good business plan, you should reverse engineer it, once you set it up and work from the end goal backwards and figure out how to do it, right? So, that's exactly what you're talking about here.

Joe: Exactly.

Jim: That's awesome. So I guess the end of the question is the marketing. What you're talking about then here was sending the letters. Sending letters to the buyers first really, right? Go through the list of who's bought ... You could use a lesser public record data to see who has been buying in the last six months. Send those people letters. I guess that would be your marketing strategy is direct market to people that are buying right now. Find out what they're buying and go find it for them, right?

Joe: Yes, exactly. You never stop marketing for buyers because your buyers may get tapped out. They may say, "You know what, I just got to stop for a little bit." Because they bought so many and they just need to finish fixing them up and getting them rented. You always got to be growing your buyers list. The thing that we did though that was really interesting is we got a bunch of buyers and then we started marketing for homes. I am a licensed realtor, but I was not doing this as a broker. I was not co-wholesaling properties. I wasn't going after these properties telling the seller, "Hey, I have a buyer for your house." I wasn't doing that. I was buying those properties for myself. I was getting them under contract for me. I was closing on them, double closing, and then turning around and selling them to my end buyers. You got to be real careful how you do it and how you phrase it. That you're not brokering. You're not putting deals, buyers, and sellers together. We did close on the deal and then we turned around and sold them.

Jim: It's cool that it's the same day but you're literally ... You're actually closing on it. I guess when you're licensed, there's probably some ethics issues involved there?

Joe: Well if you're not licensed, usually most stated have rules against brokering without a license.

There's nothing that prevents you from getting a property under contract and then selling you contract or assigning you interest in the contract to somebody else. Just something to be aware of. One of things that we did was, again, we were calling all these realtors, all these property managers, and wholesalers spreading the words in the local area groups. Just contacting every wholesaler and investor, realtor, property manager that we knew in the area, and then telling them, "Hey, we're looking for deals in this zip code that meet this criteria. If you have anything, please send it to us." We were getting their emails. Then once a week emailing everybody on our list, "Hey, do you have any deals? Do you have any deals? Do you have any deals?"

We'd mix it up, you know? We'd send out these simple one or two sentence emails every week. "Do you have any hard to sell properties? Do you have any termite damaged properties? Do you have any properties that need work? Send them our way. We'd love to … "If it's a realtor, we'd say, "You can represent us; you can get both sides of the commission, et cetera." Just by sending those weekly emails out to everybody on our list, we didn't have to do any seller marketing. We didn't have to send postcards and letters anymore. We just kept on networking with other wholesalers and realtors and they were bringing us all the deals that we could handle. It's beautiful thing when you have buyers, right? Because then you become known as the guy with deep pockets. You become known as the guy with the money who can buy the deals. Then you start getting other wholesalers bringing you their deals. You get other investors and property managers. They know you as the guy who can close. They can buy these deals and they start sending them to you.

Joe's Productivity Tip:

I'll give you two. One of them, my favorite tool on my iPhone and Mac is the application called Things. T-H-I-N-G-S. Things. It's basically just a to-do management tool, but it's really simple. It's just a way to track all your tasks, assign them to projects, and tag them. It's a pretty simple, very user friendly interface. I love Things. It's one of the things I use the most on my iPhone. What runs my entire business is Podio. Podio is a free online CRM that manages my entire business. Manages my deals, manages my coaching students, manages my administrative team and my virtual assistants. Any marketing projects that I have going on. My invoicing, expenses, time sheets, meetings. It's really, really amazing. Since I do so many deals on different markets, each market has its own workspace in Podio. It really makes it easy to manage deals in your business from anywhere in the world.

Jim: Could you spell that? Is it P-I-D-I-O?

Joe: Yup. P-O-D as in dog, I-O. Podio.com. It's a really cool too. It's free, there is a premium version that's seven dollars a month, I think. Maybe nine dollars a month. But it's really, really cool.

For more information on Joe and how he teaches people how to do this visit: www.realestateinvestingmastery.com

Matt Theriault

Matt is a 5th generation California native and a Desert Storm veteran U.S. Marine Corp.

He has worked as a full time real estate professional since 2003. After building a real estate empire using hardly one dime of his own money or one point of his own credit, mostly because he lacked both, he discovered that he had a knack for simplifying the complicated, implementing systems, and producing desirable results for himself and others.

He's just an ordinary guy who once had a goal to be a successful real estate investor and become a master of multiple streams of passive income, the concept there. The last five years he's completed, get this, more than 500 real estate transactions and amassed a portfolio of 240 rental units, so this guy is a true rock star.

He now has money, yet he hardly ever uses it on his own transactions, and the great part is he now teaches people how to do it via his popular podcast called Epic Real Estate Investing.

Matt's Answer:

Without much money is the key point there because there are probably two paths I'd go if I had money or if I didn't. But without much money I would get started the exact same way that I did. Fortunately, I found the right way the first time. I say the right way, but a way that worked, because I had almost nothing when I got started.

What I started to do was I would go to real estate investor club meetings, and I would just sit there in the audience and look for the people. I'd watch the wants and needs section where people got up in front of the room and presented what they were looking for or what they had to sell, and I connected with those people.

I just went up to them after those meetings and asked them, "Hey, if I were able to find you a buyer, would there be a referral fee in it for me?" When I found those certain investors that were agreeable to that agreement, I just asked them, "Hey, can you email me some stuff on the property and email me a picture?" I just wanted to create my own flyers. I created my own flyers with my own calls to action, my own phone number, my own email, all my own contact information.

Then I went to other real estate investor club meetings, and I got up there in front of the microphone with the needs and wants section and presented their properties. I also did that, went to just different types of networking events like Chamber of Commerce, stuff like that, and would go there and represent myself as I sell discount real estates. That worked really well for me.

I was able to connect with a wholesaler who had a large inventory, and I helped him sell a bunch of those right in the beginning. I don't know, I probably did maybe six or seven in that first month at 3000 bucks a pop, and there I was sitting on 20 grand inside of my first, I don't know, probably 45 days in the business, and then it took off.

Jim: No marketing really, right? Just some time it sounds like.

Matt: Exactly. Exactly. I still recommend that today. It's not necessarily the fastest way to do it, but I think it's a really solid way if you are limited on money. Doing the real estate with no money and no credit, that's the easy part. It's generating the lead with no money, and this is the best way that I had found to do it and probably the most sure way.

I found it did a few things. It built a buyer's list for me. It did find referrals of the stressed sellers for me. It just positioned me as a person that was in the game, playing the game. It put me up in front of the room with the microphone, and people looked at me like, 'Hey ...' I was out there doing deals.

I was really doing real estate. When you find yourself in those meetings and you have enough conversations ... When you're in there and you're not doing deals, it seems like everybody is doing deals, but once you do a deal or two, all of a sudden all of those people you thought were doing deals are now coming up to you asking you for advice. It works on very many different levels with that strategy.

Jim: You could say this is networking for deals essentially, right, because it was just building relationships with people, using their inventory to sell to other people, and it's all really built on networking, it sounds like.

Matt: Exactly. Exactly. I made money by getting in between buyers and sellers, but I also really positioned myself in front of my network as a person that was a mover and a shaker I guess, for lack of a better word, a lack of a better word than I can think of right now but, yeah, it just created me in the eyes of my peers that I was someone out there doing deals. Then the guys that are doing deals are the ones that come up and approach you to help you sell their properties, and it builds a strong network quickly.

Jim: The end of this is what marketing strategy would you focus on, but it sounds like that's wrapped into one, right? Your marketing strategy is the

	same as your initial approach, because that's how you found the initial properties to sell when you were selling other people's properties.
Matt:	Exactly. I guess they are one and the same for sure.

Matt's Productivity Tip:

After doing so many deals, you start finding tasks that are, they're time consuming, they're tedious, and they take you away from your own money making activities. One thing I latched onto right away was the use of virtual assistance. I started to delegate, say, the creating my artwork on my flyers, working on my website, stuff like that.

That's the one productivity tool that I use and I still use today. I think I've got probably 15, 16 virtual assistants that work for me now and, yeah, I think that's the one that has paid the most dividend.

Jim:	Finding these VAs, do you go to … Are there special websites? Are we just talking Elance? Or Fiverr even has a lot of them now. Do you find them on those kinds of websites?
Matt:	No, I'm actually a big fan of oDesk. I think Elance actually owns them now, but I like oDesk's platform. You can find them so cheap. One thing I did, the mistake I made in the beginning was I'd hire … I'd find someone for $3.50, hire

them to do a job, and was totally dissatisfied with it.

That was a very frustrating process, but now what I've learned to do, I'll have one job. I'll find four or five VAs at 3 to $4, hire them all to do the same job, and then pick the one I like the best and make that one a permanent member of my team.

For more information on Matt and his training program visit:

www.EpicQuickTips.com

Danny Johnson

Danny Johnson is from the blog Flipping Junkie and he's the founder of Lead Propeller, which is a real-estate investor website company and also REI Mobile, a software system for real-estate investors. He's also the author of bestselling book on Amazon called Flipping Houses Exposed, and of course Danny has flipped hundreds of properties and also wholesaled over the last decade with his wife in the San Antonio, Texas market. Danny thanks for being with us today.

Danny's Answer:

Well, basically, with what I know now and really working on being successful and flipping houses and in business in general with the software and everything I do also, I've learned, over time, about the 80-20 Principle, the Pareto Principle, which is where 20% of what you do basically generates 80% of the results. So the people that are super successful— because everybody's got the same 24 hours in a day, and there's a lot of people who seem to get a lot more done in that same 24 hours than other people. So if you think about why that is possible, and yeah, some people leverage money–they've got the money so they can leverage that–but for the most part, what the successful people do is really look at everything and focus on the things that are going to generate the biggest results in the shortest amount of time and with the littlest effort. So being asked that question I think I would sit down and figure out exactly what those things are, what's the 20%? I'm not going to spend my time sitting there trying to design a business card for a week, the perfect business card for my new house buying business. And I say that—

It's the whole comfort zone thing; we're in our comfort zone, we don't want to get out of it. My wife has always been really good about kicking me out of my comfort zone, like, "What are you doing designing that logo still?! Get out there and do something!" So I spent all that time designing those flyers and the logo and stuff and I get them made and they just sit in my office. But that's what I would get past now, that I've already moved out of the comfort zone. But for new people, that's really what should be focused on, getting out of the comfort zone and doing these things that are the 20%, because that's the way to success because most people know that most new businesses fail and I think a lot of it has to do with that. So that's kind of a vague answer, but I can go into exactly what it is that I would do with 20%, but if you think about it, leveraging other people finding deals for you is really one of the best ways to be efficient, get the most out of your energy and time.

Basically, the way I would start that is I would start by trying to find the most successful, active real-estate investors in my area. So what I would do is I would find an agent that can look up properties that were bought for cash within the last three to six months, and then find out who those people were, looking up the e-records and stuff like that and find out who those people were buying all those properties and you'll start to see the same names over and over again, and if you can get in touch with them, usually there will be a mailing or something, send a letter saying you want to talk to them. You can also find out a lot about who the real successful, active investors are at the REIA Meetings, the Real-Estate Investor Association Meetings, and when you get there most people just kind of want to keep to themselves and sit there and listen and stuff like that, but you just gotta push yourself out of that and talk to people, and when you start talking to people and asking around, "So who in town is buying a lot of houses right now?" And you'll start to hear the same names over and over again.

So those are the kind of people that you spend your time trying to get to know. It's not like I'm going up to them and saying, "Hey, teach me this or that, show me what you're doing to get these deals." The key there is just to find out what they want. I would want to provide value for them.

Jim: So we're going out there finding the cash buyers who are buying right now and basically ask them: "Hey, what are you buying? What would be the best thing to bring to you if you were looking to buy something? What would it be?" So you're going to bring them what they're looking for, right?

Danny: Right. And I'm considering all of this as if I didn't have money to buy houses. I'd want to start with wholesaling and getting to know these people, and the wholesaling doesn't have to be long term. It's just to get your foot in the door, get experience, and to get these connections. I would ask them: what are you looking for? What types of properties have you been buying or selling and where? What parts of town? What's your favorite? Someone called you with a deal and you asked where it was, where would you want them to say it was? What would get you excited? I would say, "What do you use to determine if that's a deal or not? What kind of numbers do you want to see?" Basically, when you meet these guys and you talk to them and you get this information from them, of course you've got to write it down. You can't just think you're going to remember all of that. So you write it all down; you don't just sit there and ask them a bunch of questions that you could get the answer to online. Don't waste their time. But just really quickly introduce yourself and everything and find out what they want and then the key is to go and try to find that stuff, try to find those deals.

So how do you do that? What's the best use of your time for doing that? What's the 20% for finding the deals? Basically, one of those things is to find a hungry agent, like a real-estate agent, and what you'll do is have them submit offers on distressed properties. You might be concerned about, "Well, what if they accept their offer and it was too much?" Or this and that. And basically, once you know their criteria for what they're looking for and the areas they're looking for, you can determine—with the help of the agent of value—that the house would be resold at. From there you can use those investor's criteria to figure out what an offer would be and then you just offer a little lower than that. So you get these offers out there, and then 99.9 times out of 100, the banks and the distressed sellers are going to counter, because usually it's a low offer. So if you're kind of uncertain about it, about what kind of amounts you're offering, when that counter offer comes, then you get the investor/buyer, the serious cash buyer investor involved, and say, "Look, I've got this deal that countered at this price, can ballpark." So then you've already got a buyer ready to buy the deal from you.

You can do a double-close or something like that. There's different ways to do it and that's just one of them. The thing about the agent is if you get comfortable enough in this and you start to make this work and you know, after doing a couple of talking with the successor investors, they're telling you what exactly they're wanting to buy and how much. It becomes a lot easier to know: this is the price for that house. Then from there you can develop the system where you've got the agent doing the looking for you and determining those things too, so you don't even have to do it. So they could be like keeping the eye, putting the filters on the MLS and the reminders and notices where they get the system to tell them when new properties come up in those areas, and then they can determine the offers and submit them for you.

Obviously, you'll want this to be a really good system that's documented and you know the agent's not offering too much, like at first you can verify what they offer before they submit or something like that, but you want to get it to the point where you're building that system while they're doing those things for you and the only time they contact you is when they get a counter that's within a ballpark. So there's nothing that says you can't do that with more than one agent. You could go out and try to find three or four agents and build a relationship. Obviously, you're going to have people that say they want to do it but they don't take action; the realtor drags their feet and takes two days to submit and offer or something and you don't want that.

So you find the ones that are willing to hustle, and they know it's going to take more work in the beginning before you see any results, but if they're really hungry, they can see into how that can progress and become a profitable thing for them, be willing to do the work. So that's a way to leverage your time and to do the 20%. Not just with agents either, though; this whole thing, working like that, can be done with wholesalers as well. Wholesalers, people that go out and basically do what you're doing but selling to the other investors that have the cash to buy it, fix it, sell it. So you just build the relationship with those wholesalers and try to get them sending you the deals that they find, so now you've got agents, you've got wholesalers looking for deals for you.

Obviously, the really good wholesalers, they typically already have some buyers that are really good, so it's kind of hard sometimes to get in the door to get them to see the deals, but if you go into there thinking that it won't actually happen, you won't actually try to build those relationships, but I know for a fact, if you keep trying and you're able to really take the deals down, then you will start getting those deals from wholesalers. That's what I would focus on and then obviously, being that I'm into real-estate investor websites, I would go ahead and set one of those up and spend time trying to get that to a rank because once you do that, you start getting those leads yourself, the cost isn't—

There's certain areas that there is a lot of competition with the websites, but most people don't spend enough time trying to promote them, so if you're the one that persistent, you get up there in rank and it's not all that difficult to do.

We set up some things so that they get a response back right away, and then since you get to notice, you also get a text yourself when a lead comes in so that you're able to contact them right away. We have a two-step process on the pages where they don't just come to site and see this huge form. "Aw man, I don't want to fill that out. It's asking everything about everything on there." It's just got the basic information, their name, number, email address, an address, and when they submit that, then it takes them to the longer form, but when they submitted that short form is when you get the text, so you know instantly, as soon as somebody's sitting on your website and they're looking, even if they're just considering filling out the longer form, you could already be calling them.

So the guy that's got the website that he's just getting notification in his email or something, if he doesn't have something checking that email right away, he might not know about it for a while and the people have already gone to three or four websites.

Jim: So where do they find information on your website?

Danny: It's leadpropeller.com.

Danny's Productivity Tip:

Well, what I've been using a lot lately is called Trello. It's a free web software. It's Trello.com. You just sign up for a free account or whatever and then it's basically just a to-do list card system, and you can set up multiple ones of these. I have a personal one, a business one, different projects and everything like that. So you have these cards, like a list for to-do and then doing and then doing. So your to-do list basically becomes a list of all the stuff to do and then you can easily drag and drop and re-arrange things so that you can make the list of all the things you'd think that you'd need or would want to do and then sit there and sort them by what's going to be the 20%. What's going to get you the most results with the least effort? And move that sucker up to the top because that's what you want to do first.

You just kind of do this weekly because you know as well as I do, entrepreneurs are always getting ideas, writing them down, and losing them, but you can just go to this thing and you can get an app for the phone for free that also ties into it so it's all synched everywhere and you just can go and add this idea to your to-do list and then every week, sit there and re-arrange them again and think through what's going to get you the most results, and then force yourself to pull the top ones from the to-do list to the doing list so that whenever you're focused, you're not focused on this giant to-do list. You're only focused on the one or two items you've got on the doing list until they're done, and then you move them to done, go back to the to-do list and for the top again the 20% stuff.

To check out more on Danny and see his blog visit:

www.flippingjunkie.com

WENDY PATTON

Wendy is the nation's leading expert on lease options and how to put $5-10,000 in your bank account in the next 29 days. She was a former struggling single mother who quickly went from broke to accumulating millions of dollars in real estate.

She has over 28 years' experience as a full-time real estate investor. She's done rehabs, multi family, land development, pre-construction, foreclosures, subject to, commercial. Actually, she's done a lot in the real estate industry, but she primarily likes to focus on no money or little money down and has done hundreds of lease-option transactions. Hundreds.

She's a published author of 5 best sellers on creative seller financing and lease options, 4 in the US and 1 in the UK. She's the founder of Michigan Real Estate Investors Association and has appeared on HGTV's My House Is Worth What? Wendy, thank you for being here today.

Wendy's Answer:

That's a great question because everyone of course always thinks, "Oh, you would do lease options right away." I do think lease options are one of the very, very best ways for new investors to get involved or people without money or credit.

It's definitely one of the few strategies that you can use for that situation, but I would say ... Let me just back that thought up a little bit. I do think it's really great if someone starts investing when they're broke. I'll tell you why. I think it's really good because you have to be creative and you have to figure out how to do this business without money.

I think that's so important that you don't need a lot of money. As you grow your business, of course, then you can start using more and more money for different marketing strategies and to really build it to a much bigger scale. If I was looking back, I would probably say I wish I had learned how to be a good wholesaler when I first started investing.

The reason for that is, number 1, it teaches you how to source deals. It really teaches you how to find the golden nugget and how to negotiate and evaluate a deal that's good enough to flip it to somebody else. You get really, really good at finding deals. It's very low overhead, very low risk, no tenants, no toilets, none of that stuff. I think I would say wholesaling.

As a wholesaler, what marketing strategy would you focus on to find those deals? Where would you direct your efforts? With little money, "Okay, we're going to wholesale," what kind of marketing would you do or where would you focus your time?

Wendy: That's what's really cool. There are so many possibilities for that with wholesaling. I would probably focus on yellow letters, but I would probably target a group like either probate, divorce, some kind of situation like back taxes. In my state, some of the wholesalers that I buy from ... Coincidentally, that's how I buy them all ..., They tend to go after probate. They tend to go after the back taxes.

I think that those have ended up being really good sources for a couple of my best wholesalers that I buy from. I've never switched to that. I do my thing. Wholesaling is great for options too because you can wholesale a lease option.

Wholesalers that sometimes can't structure a deal good enough to put to another investor, if they figure out how to wholesale a lease option, they can still structure a deal with that owner and flip it to an in-tenant buyer. Very different exit strategy and a different buyer, but potentially it's just as much money for those deals that don't have enough equity in them to just flip them to someone else.

Jim: You're probably just pulling out then the down, the non-refundable option money, I would imagine. Is that how we're making our money there?

Wendy: You got it. You're usually 3-5% down. A $200,000 home, even if seller owes 200 and it's worth 200, a wholesaler can't do anything with it, but they really could on an option. They can absolutely flip that to someone for probably 205/210 and take 5 to 10 grand out of that deal, and everybody is happy. It wouldn't be to an investor. It would be to a person that's going to live in it.

Jim: Where would they be selling it to? To the end buyer the person that hopefully satisfies the option at the end and then everybody cashes out then.

Wendy: At least in my state, you can buy the back tax list from the county. Then of course the probate you can buy lists from a lot of different list providers if you just Google buying a mailing list. A lot of times, yellow letter companies also provide the list service as well. You tell them, "Yeah, this is a yellow letter I want you to use and here is the kind of group and area and zip code. I want it." They'll do it all for you.

Wendy's Productivity Tip:

I would say one of the key things for me is, every year, I always set my goals. Between Christmas and New Year, I set my goals for the next year. I really break those down, let's say, if I want to do X number of deals, make $X.

Then what I do is I start breaking that down by what do I need to do this month? What do I need to do this week? What do I need to do today? Every day, I have a list of ... I don't know if you've read Gary Keller's The One Thing. A great book, The One Thing.

Jim: Yeah, it is a great book.

Wendy: I actually have his list from that book that I use every day, which is my success list and my to do list. The success list are the things that are going to help get you to towards your goals. The to do list, if they don't get done, you're not going to die today. The success list are the key things that you must get done that day. They're the most important things. I really try to ... Every day, I have a list. Every day. Every day, I have a list.

I mean 7 days a week, even if it's at home. Even if I'm at home for a Saturday or Sunday or a day off, I'll still have a list unless I'm on vacation. I have a list of here's what ... Even if it's personal. "Am I going to clean the bathroom today? I'm going to make sure I call my mom and my aunt." It's personal things too that I always try to make sure those things are on the list.

Jim: Write things down to accomplish your goals, whatever they are, personal or whatever. If you

	don't write them down, they're probably not going to get done.
Wendy:	You've got it. It's very simple. It's not one of those complex things that costs a lot of money for productivity tools, but it's the basics.
Jim:	That's a lot of what ... I've been asking this to everybody I've interviewed in this series and a lot of it has been simple easy stuff. When I started asking that question, I didn't know the responses I would get from people achieving at a high level, like the people in this interview series. It's been more basic stuff.

A couple of guys have had their ... They're tech guys so they had technology things, but most people, it was from setting goals and sticking to them to weekly goals to, like you just said, breaking down ... Set your goals and then reverse engineer them so that you can break them down to what you need to do on a daily basis to achieve those.

It's been really cool to see that you don't have to reinvent the wheel and have some crazy productivity happen, but how about just writing down and setting your goals and actually reading them daily and doing them. How about that? Something as simple as that that anybody could do, anybody should be doing?

Wendy:	You've got it, Jim. I should say too though that one of the things ... I don't know if you call this

productivity tool or what, but one of the things for every investor ... I own a real estate office too, and, of course, my realtor is exactly the same thing.

It's any business owner, one key thing that they need to do every day is prospect. It's building ... If you're an investor, it's building a buyers' list, a sellers' list. It's going after deals. It's every day. It's got to be every day.

Until you have too many sellers or too many buyers or too many of whatever it is you're trying to go after, that's your only focus. It should be every day. I prospect in my different businesses every day. It's something I do every day for a couple of hours every day. That is key. That's what truly will build wealth when you do this. It's consistency over and over and over again.

For more information on Wendy and lease options visit:

www.WendyPatton.com

Joe Fairless

Joe is founder of Fairless Investing and he controls over 7 million in real estate. He's also the host of a top-rated investing podcast called Best Real Estate Investing Advice Ever which is awesome. He started investing in real estate in 2009 when he still had a full time job like a lot of us. He was working in a New York City advertising agency. He made the switch to apartments. He started with single family stuff but he made the switch to apartments when he realized he could achieve his financial goals faster buying a lot more homes or units as it were, all at once.

He has raised millions in capital and is currently working on a 400-unit development. That's right, 400-unit development. Joe consults beginning investors that want to buy apartments and buy apartment communities and how to raise money from investors in order to do that.

Joe's Answer:

The first thing I would do is I would focus on an asset class and that assess class would be multifamily. The reason why is because of the industry trends and where I believe we're headed from a population standpoint, from the amount of new construction units that were not happening a couple years ago. We certainly have a lot of new construction now but we still have about three to five years to catch up.

If I were to start my real estate company over right now, I'd focus on multifamily and then I would focus on buying multifamily with other people's money because as you mentioned in the question, if I had very little amount of money of my own, then obviously I'll need to partner with other people. In order to do that quite simply, I would need investors or I would need to provide help from a time or work, sweat labor standpoint or sweat equity rather, although it's probably one and the same, to someone who is out there doing it and who has the capital and I would provide value in their life and get in on a deal with them or bring in investors of my own and syndicate a deal. Raise money and buy a multifamily apartment community.

Jim: When you say like use other people's money, like with private investors, it's not necessarily with big private groups, right? It could just be somebody with money, right? Like a friend or family member, somebody that has money to invest that's sitting in a bank account, correct? It doesn't have to be like you have to go approach some scary big investment firm, correct?

Joe: That's correct and I actually have not approached some big scary investment firm.

I've only worked with people who I have a relationship with who are looking to invest in something other than what they're currently doing which tends to be stocks and bonds. Approaching them with an opportunity that I confidently believe in and am inspired by and helping them make more money than they're currently making.

Jim: Wow! That's great. When you're saying multifamily, are we talking like... I mean, obviously we mentioned in your intro that you're doing like a 400-unit which might blow some people away that are listening and they're going to be reading this in the e-book. Multifamily could be 10 or 20, right? I mean it doesn't have to be 400. I don't want to intimidate the people that are listening and reading here.

Joe: Yeah. I mean, it could be anything above five or five and above is a different type of loan. It's a commercial loan. Than anything two through four is also multifamily because it's multiple families living under one roof. If it was me personally, if I had the same knowledge, if I'm not completely starting from scratch with the relationships, then I would start ... If I had to do my business over, I would start with a couple hundred units but someone who hasn't done a deal before, you could do it as small as you want. It's just a matter of finding the right partner and structuring in a way that makes sense for you and then.

Jim: As far as finding these apartment complexes whether it be 4 or 400 units, what's the best marketing strategy? Like knowing what you know now, where would you go to find these deals? What marketing strategy would you say would be something you could go back to that's been very effective?

Joe: Yeah. The number one thing ... you did ask what marketing strategy would I focus on and I wholeheartedly believe in relationships, friendships, so let me be very specific with the marketing strategy. What I would do is I would... as you mentioned, I am the host of a popular investing podcast and that podcast has allowed me to meet so many people all across the nation doing incredibly interesting stuff. I imagine, Jim, that you came across me because of that podcast.

I would ... the marketing strategy would simply be, I would create my own podcast. I would interview successful people and through those interviews I would establish relationships with brokers all across the country. I would become a thought leader for potential investors to invest in my deals and I would continually learn along the way. By the way, all this stuff I'm saying, "I would," I'm actually living and breathing and doing it right now so I know that's an effective of doing all three of those things.

Joe's Productivity Tip:

The first thing I do without fail every single morning is I drink a liter of water that has a scoop of Tony Robins green supplement in it. It's just like all organic. Spinach, alfalfa leaves, wheat grass. The first thing I do to start off the day. It alkalizes my body and it liquidates me and hydrates me and I literally ... this is kind of crazy, but I literally ... my eyes are opening up as I drink more and more of that whenever I first wake up. It literally just wakes me up and gets me started, ready to start the day.

For more information on Joe:

http://www.fairlessinvesting.com/

GARRETT GUNDERSON

Garrett is a champion at finding spendable cash for real estate investors and entrepreneurs without having to work harder, take more risks or increase your overhead. He has dedicated his career to debunking many of the widely accepted myths and fabrications that undermine the prosperity and joy of millions of hardworking IS business owners. Gunderson's company Wealth Factory empowers entrepreneurs to build sustainable wealth through financial efficiency, organization leading to clarity and peace of mind and financial comp. His firm was named the Inc 500. And you may recognize him from the NY Times bestselling book "Killing Sacred Cows" or one of his many appearances as a guest on CNBC, Fox News, ABC and many other of the news outlets.

Garrett's Answer:

I don't really believe that it takes money to make money, so it wouldn't matter necessarily how much I have or not starting over, because I have this formula. The formula is: if you want more financial capital that's a byproduct. It's the byproduct of two more precious forms of capital or resources, the first one being mental capital. Mental capital is your unique knowledge, wisdom, it's ideas, it's ... just anything that you really know and then when you take that, and apply it to relationship capital, which are people, networks, organizations, subscribers, buyers, you name it, it's people. The formula out there is your mental capital times your relationship capital is what determines your financial capital.

So, if I was starting over, I would say, what is it that I know in the world of real estate that I could share with others? Whether that's through a white paper, or even launching a book, because it doesn't take a lot of money to launch a book these days with all the different self-publishing platforms that are out there and all the systems. I would start providing massive value with the unique knowledge that I had sharing success stories, sharing failures and lessons, and then sharing current market things that are going on in a valuable way that people would gravitate towards. They could become my bird dog, they could become my strategic partners, they could become my students, they could become buyers. Whatever it is, I would start building up a big subscriber base and a big database of people with that mental capital so that now with all that relationship capital, I would have massive opportunity to go out there and do something. I could learn from them, I could share with them. That's where I think a lot of people try to do it too much alone or they don't have enough of a support network, or they're not putting those ideas out there that really make them critically think though what they're up to. That's the formula that I would apply. The first thing I would do is start being a thought leader in the space, creating value and content.

Jim: So maybe ... learning yourself and if you're starting out and trying to learn the business, you pick up a specific strategy and learn everything there is to know about it, is that kind of what I'm getting from you? Then become someone who is published or maybe even teaches on it, because you've learned that so well.

Garrett: Absolutely. Look, you're ... I don't know if you're saying if I was starting over or if I had never done a real estate transaction, I'm looking at, look, the very first real estate transaction I ever did, I was 19 years old and I bought a house, used a CHamp loan for a down payment. Rented it out to some other people, while I still lived there during my college years. Then, my next real estate deal, I actually funded escrow to acquire a property and we turned around and just sold it. I basically doubled my money in three months. I used my wife's credit on another deal, and we bought a property, then I got in a partnership. Along the way, I had plenty of success stories but I also I have plenty of danger signs, and warnings and issues that people don't plan for.

I mean, I have sold properties by getting a few hundred people to go through an open house in one day, and then I auctioned the property off at the end of the day. That's something that I could teach people about, and they would be pretty interested in because it was relatively unique. We've fractionalized property before, and when we fractionalized it we were able to basically, have more people get in and buy in without as much of payment, when lending became an issue in 2008, for awhile.

I would bring in experts that teach about credit, I would even do what you're doing and interview other people that could share different things. I would really build up a big following, and that's a great excuse to interview people and learn what they know, and then translate to the different people that are out there because, maybe that's a strategy that you'd want to apply or you'd want to partner on. It's such an abundant opportunity. Regardless of whether you have a dollar to invest or not today, you have your mental capital. You better make sure you have good mental capital and you have relationship capital. You better be continually

	building that by providing value, solving problems and serving those people.
Jim:	That's awesome. So essentially what you're saying ... is an advanced networking strategy you're talking about. At the end of the day, you're talking about networking with other investors. I think a lot of people are scared when they get into business, because you start on your own, and you're like, 'I can't talk to other investors in my area, they are my competition!' This is going against that, hey, you should talk to those people because they're in your network and you never know. We're stronger in numbers, is that kind of what you were getting at?
Garrett:	Yeah, let me give a real life example of what I did. In 1998, I entered the financial services business. What I did was ... I wasn't married at the time, I was still going to college, and I was actually making more than my professors were just doing financial services, so I had a lot of time, because school was relatively easy, certain semesters were. I was travelling, and gaining a lot of information and a lot of knowledge and then I started to present that at study groups

that these financial people would do. Then they would start bringing me into the cases and doing joint work. I created a program where they could come in and watch me do things for a day or two, a shadowing program and pay for it. People that had been in the business for 30 years were coming to find out what this young kid was doing and making good money, and had different strategies. Then I started doing a conference call twice a month. A one-time live event. We were getting tons of financial people to show up. At first I was doing it free, and then eventually I started charging $160 a month for it, and then launching the shadowing program.

Here's what happened, instead of saying, "oh you're training your competition" what happened is, if they ever ran into a case that was difficult they brought me in because they knew my expertise. Or if they ever ran into someone who was already my client, they said great things about me rather than to try take that client away from me. Most people think and scarcely far too often, they hoard information, they cut back, and they don't share. They think they've got this little secret. The problem is, if you're in that situation, you stop operating at full capacity. If you abundantly share, and you give the very best you have to offer, it's going to help you stretch and take you further. And other people want to give back because a law of reciprocity. I'll admit there are some people that are scoundrels and are just going to rake whatever information they can from you. You can protect yourself and stop spending time with them.

But if you operate from an abundant mindset, you share that, they're going to want to share the best they have to offer and all of a sudden you expand your mental capital, you build a much better relationship. When you create massive value for someone they want to do things for you. If you hold back, it kills the relationship. Networking, far too often, is about what people can get versus what they can give. The people that dominate in the world of networking are the people that give massive value. Whether they charge a little bit for it or nothing for it, what they're really doing is building a Rolodex of people who go, "There's someone who knows what they're doing, who is willing to abundantly share. I would love to get to know them or provide value for them." That is a game changer.

If you apply that to the world of real estate, you'll have such an unfair advantage, you'll get access to insiders you would never had access to before. You'll be able to get people's best strategies because they want to share with you the same way you did with them. You'll end up with a team of partners or bird dogs, like I said, or whatever it is, even buyers. That's where a lot of the opportunity is going to come from.

Garrett's Productivity Tip:

So the thing that I do on a daily basis … you have to look into this and try this out to see just how it's a productivity strategy. I start my day with three "E"s. I get up, and I'm exercising four days a week. I used to do more, but what I found is rest is just as important as the work out. Exercise, or reading about, or setting up my health.

That's the first E, exercise. The second one is education. Before I start my day, I take some time to listen to something or read something. I don't care if it's 10 minutes, or if it's 30 minutes, or if it's just while you're driving in to go do something, you're making sure to saturate your mind with good information in something that you want to know, that you can apply out there in the world that you're even passionate about. And the third E, I'm going to learn the term enlightenment. Whatever it is that gets you in the right mindset so you can be more abundant for the day. For some, it's a simple gratitude exercise. For me, I like to do a little mediation. For some, it might just be having a little quiet and thinking time. For some it might be more of a spiritual type of thing, like prayer or reading something.

But if you start your day with 3 "E"s, exercise, education, enlightenment, you're going to be more abundant. You're going to be able to handle the difficult situations and you're going to have a different of energy because you invested in yourself before you go out and do anything else. So the 3 "E"s, I call it doing your power hour before the day starts.

Jim:	Wow, that's awesome. I read an article years ago that said, the most successful people, entrepreneurs, business people in the world get up three hours before they're going to leave the house for the day. The average person actually gets up an hour before they leave the house for the day. Obviously, you can't get up

an hour before you're going to leave for the day if you're going to power hour first thing in the morning ... that's powerful stuff. Obviously, that's why you've been producing at a high level for a very long time because you've practiced that kind of stuff.

Garrett: Thanks, man. I got to tell you, it's especially effective in difficult times. Or when you're dealing with a whole bunch, or you feel like you don't have the time. It makes the other 23 hours of the day more beneficial, more productive, and more worthwhile. Even though you're taking an hour from your day, it's kind of like you're physically nourished, you're mentally nourished, and you're showing up with a different level of intention and energy. It's absolutely worth it.

Stephen Covey wrote about this in one of his first books in the 70s where he talked about if you take 30 minutes before you go out for the day and do simply what I'm talking about here, the other 23.5 hours operated much more effectively. It's not about the amount of time, when we're talking about productivity; it's an inverse relationship with time and effort. It means, yes, you're spending the time away from things you could go out and do, like email or talking to customers, or finding bills. But when you show up to do those things, you're just going to have much more clarity, much more energy, much more power and it'll make you much, much more productive.

For more information on Garrett and his company visit:

www.WealthFactory.com

Jim Huntzicker

I have been a real estate investor in Northern Illinois since 2007. I am also a licensed real estate agent (IL) and have been since 2006. I started out as an aggressive new agent helping investors buy and sell their rehab properties. I quickly realized I was on the wrong side of that transaction and that is when I decided to become a real estate investor myself. These days my primary focus as an investor is rehabbing. I buy, renovate and sell residential properties in Chicago and its suburbs. Since I got into the real estate business I have been involved in over 450 transactions. My real estate investing company is Yellow Star Properties, LLC and we do 10-14 rehabs at any one time.

In 2011 I started coaching for a big national real estate investing education company. It was great and I truly got so much out of coaching the students. Some were brand new and I would help them get their first deal and others were seasoned investors looking for new ways and systems to help grow and automate their existing businesses. The reason I decided to start coaching in the first place was selfishly to be able to attend their private coaches only mastermind event they hold twice a year. Though over time the company grew so much that it just wasn't really one-on-one coaching anymore and was more of a corporate environment and it just was no longer a good fit for me. After about a year passed, I found I really missed coaching and advising others to help them reach their real estate investing goals. I then decided to start my own, true one-on-one coaching group known now as RealEstateInvestorAcademy.com. I only work with a very small group of students because of the intense one-on-one time this requires in order to produce results. Due to the high demand for my coaching program and since I couldn't take everyone in I started a group coaching program too. This is a great, intimate, small group environment in which to interact with other investors from all over the country. You get to ask your own questions and hear questions that other investors are asking too. This always adds a ton of insight to all of the members in the group. RealEstateInvestorAcademy.com is where I teach real estate investors how to take their business to a whole new level. For more info on this go to www.RealEstateInvestorAcademy.com

Jim's Answer:

This is a great question and that is exactly why I asked it to all of these bad asses (respectively). You see, I am a rehabber and have been since I started 7 years ago. I have used the Multiple Listing Service (MLS) as my primary deal source the entire time and still do. 75% of the deals I do come straight out of the MLS. Since I was a real estate agent first I had a very good understanding of how to use the MLS. Now using it as an investor and an agent was night and day but I knew how it all worked. Check out www.MLS Domination.com for more details on how to do that.

First of all this is not easy money and the info contained in the book is in no way, shape or form a "get rich quick" guide. This is however a step-by-step blue print to making millions (you heard me, millions) of dollars as a real estate investor. Anything you can make a lot of money at never comes easy. If it was easy everyone would do it and we would not be able to cash such large check. First of all you need to pick a niche and stick with it and master it. Wholesaling is a great place to start because you can do it with literally no money. Then you need to start networking at the Real Estate Investors clubs in the area. Figure out who the real players are and figure out how to make them you mentor. Even if you have to pay them you need to find a way. You can't expect to get somewhere you've never been by doing the same things you have always done. The first real estate investing course I took was $10,000 and I put the entire thing on my credit card because I knew I needed the training but didn't have the money. Knowing what I do now I would pay $30,000 for that training because it taught me the tips and tricks it would have taken me years to learn on my own and would have cost me a lot more in real world "training" than the actual course cost itself.

You also need to find the biggest wholesalers in your market and start selling their properties; this is also known as Co-wholesaling. You need to get their permission to market their properties but most will have no issue with that. There, now you have some inventory to sell. You can take that inventory across town to a different REIA and offer it as a property for sale. None of this costs money, just a little time and initiative.

Also, for the cash buyers I would find a public record service. In Illinois, ours is called Record-Info-Services. You can get any public record you want from these people for a fee. However, if you have no money you can always walk into the county recorders office and look through the public recorder. Anyone can do it. That's why it's called a public record. You want to pull all of the cash sales in the last 3 months. Then you should send them a letter or try to get their number. Google them... whatever it takes.

Once you get ahold of them you find out exactly what they want and then go find it for them. You can use other wholesalers as bird dogs or you can use realtors as bird dogs. I would call everyone and anyone who works in those areas and start shaking trees for property.

Speaking of realtors, now we've come to the MLS which is an awesome deal source and is my personal favorite. There are so many angles for this strategy I came up with a course called MLS Domination to teach you more about them. You can see the free training at www.MLSDomination.com.

As you can see from several of the responses there are, several ways to do real estate investing without any of your own money or credit and little to no risk BUT you need to learn how to do that. So do whatever it takes to hire a mentor. Look into the guys, and gal in this book; most of them have some sort of training program. In fact many of them offer awesome free training on their websites. You need to find a mentor that is a good fit for you and your personality. Not everyone is a good fit to work together. Take me for instance: I teach investors 1 on 1 and how I start out that process is a free, 1 hour consultation (after application has been filled out) and I am giving my best ideas and advice for that person's business but I am also feeling them out to see if they are a good fit to work with me. You see, my coaching program is for existing investors who want to take their business to the next level. It is a 3 month program that is $15,000 and there is no turning back once we start. You will need about $3-5,000 more for marketing material after the fact. Knowing this, you can understand why I need to make sure it is a good fit. And every time I open enrollment I turn down a few people that are willing to give me their money because I can tell we are not going to mesh. I have a very rapid personality and work at a pretty fast pace and that is not for everyone. I talk fast and I act fast so if you talk a bit slower and act a bit slower and really need to think about your decisions for a long time, engineers need not apply sorry, I will still be able to add value to you but we would not be the best fit.

Why am I telling you about this? First, it's because I just opened enrollment for this program again and can only take on a handful of people due to the intense 1 on 1 time with me. Secondly, to let you know the people I work with are already successful investors that are still reaching out to get more help in order to take their business to the next level. I still have and always will have mentors in my life. I look at it as forced accountability and if you don't want that then maybe a 9-5 job is better for you. It is like working out with a personal trainer; I can work out just fine on my own but every time I work out with my trainer he pushes me past my comfort zone (every single time). To apply go to www.JimHuntzicker.com

Jim's Productivity Tip:

I will be very short on this because it has had such a tremendous impact on my business and it is so easy to do yet most people cannot bring themselves to do it. And that is time-blocking. No phone, no texting, no email, no anything other than what I am working on. I do this for a minimum of 2 hours and most days it is 3 hours a day. I easily get as much done in those 3 hours as I used to all day. Turn your phone OFF. Shut your email down. Just get your work done.

There is a great app that plays peaceful music and blocks your phone and computer so nothing can come through and that is Focus@will.

I will add one of the things I do first thing every morning; as soon as I wake up is splash cold water on my face. It will take a day or 2 to get use to but once you do it gives you a jump start to your day right out of the gate.

For more information on Jim and his private 1-on-1 coaching

you can visit: www.RealEstateInvestorAcademy.com

Also check out his FREE MLS training

for real estate investors at:

www.MLSDomination.com

==

Well I hope you all found this useful I know I did. You see the key is to never stop learning, never assume you already know everything there is to know. You never know when you will learn some little tip or trick that can make all the difference to your business.

I am going to leave you will a few of the quotes that are up on my goal wall at my office. These are the ones that help me when I am making a tough decision or I need to put in that extra time. It helps me remember why I am doing it and what is possible if I put my mind to it. I hope this information served you and has left you feeling as inspired as it did me.

"You will miss 100% of the shots you don't take"

—Wayne Gretzky

"Success is buried on the other side of frustration"

—Tony Robbins

"Failure defeats losers, failure inspires winners"

—Robert Kiyosaki

"If you are not willing to risk the usual, you will have to settle for the ordinary"

—Jim Rohn

"It is in your moments of decision that your destiny is shaped"

—Tony Robbins

"The difference between who you are and who you want to be is what you do"

—Anonymous

==

Another RealEstateInvestorAcademy.com | Product by Jim Huntzicker

www.ingramcontent.com/pod-product-compliance
Lightning Source LLC
Chambersburg PA
CBHW051851170526
45168CB00001B/59